Foreword

VICTORIA & ALBERT: TREASURES FROM A ROYAL MARRIAGE is the third exhibition arranged under the auspices of the Historic Lincoln Trust. Our first was in Magna Carta year, Lincolnshire's Great Exhibition and in 2017 we marked the 800th anniversary of the decisive Battle of Lincoln with Battles and Dynasties. This year we mark the 200th anniversary of the births of both Victoria and Albert with this very special exhibition which helps to underline the influence and importance of the Victorian Era and, in particular, the amazing contribution that Prince Albert, who died so tragically early, made to the cultural and scientific life of our country. We are proud to be able to show some of the early treasures of what was then the Museum of South Kensington, with its Gallery of British Art, and which we know as the Victoria & Albert Museum – so named at the Queen's insistence when it was proposed that it should be the Victoria Museum.

Our main thanks, of course, go to Dr Tristram Hunt, Director of the Victoria & Albert Museum, and his trustees for their generously lending us a large majority of the pictures and objects in this exhibition, including not only some great and fine pictures but a number of other treasures, the principal of which, is the great Gloucester Candlestick, one of the first treasures of the V&A and dating from the early twelfth century. Among the most evocative images are the earliest of our Christmas cards, for the Victorian age is perhaps most fondly remembered by many as the age when Christmas became the greatest of family festivals.

We are most grateful to Her Majesty the Queen for lending, from the Royal Collection, Winterhalter's marvellous portrait of Queen Victoria with Prince Albert Edward (later Prince of Wales and Edward VII) a charming picture which was a gift from Queen Victoria to her Prime Minister, Robert Peel, in 1846. From the National Portrait Gallery are a number of very special pictures and busts of great Victorians, including a particularly splendid portrait of the Duke of Wellington. Perhaps the most charming single object in the exhibition is the portrait of Princess Victoria aged four, kindly lent to us by the Dulwich Picture Gallery.

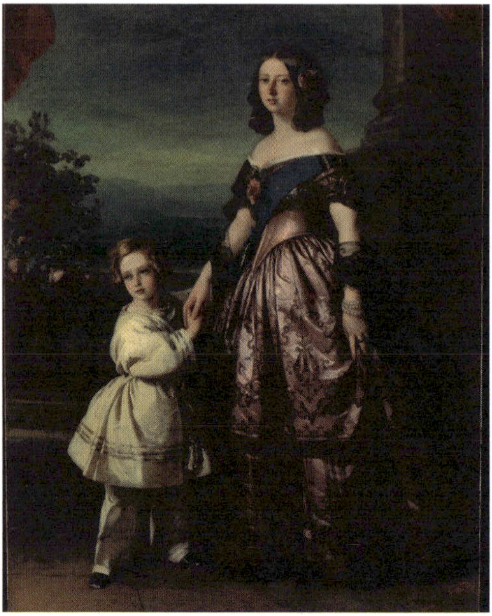

Oil on canvas, 1846.
RCIN 406945.

Queen Victoria with the Prince of Wales

Winterhalter was born in the Black Forest and studied art in Munich. In 1838 he was recommended to Queen Victoria by Queen Louise Marie of the Belgians. From 1842 until his death, he produced many portraits of the British royal family. This portrait shows the Queen with her eldest son, Albert Edward, Prince of Wales. She gave it as a Christmas present to her Prime Minister, Sir Robert Peel. In 1939 Queen Mary purchased it for the Royal Collection.

Exhibitions do not happen just because of the generosity of those who lend. We depend upon the generosity of those who are prepared to sponsor and to all our sponsors, listed elsewhere in this book, I wish to express heartfelt thanks, as I do to those individuals who have worked so hard to bring about this exhibition. Once again Dr Alan Borg, himself a former distinguished Director of the V&A, has acted as our honorary curator. And Dr Nicholas Bennett has edited and written much of this publication as he did the book of Lincolnshire's Great Exhibition and the catalogue of Battles and Dynasties.

A special word of thanks must go to Andrea Martin and her team at the Usher and the Collection for all they have done. Andrea herself has been the most diligent and efficient supervisor of all the myriad of forms that have to be completed in connection with important loans for a great exhibition and in this she has been admirably and ably assisted by Dawn Heywood.

We are very fortunate in having our Usher Gallery, deservedly a grade II* listed building and the Collection, the finest modern building in the city of Lincoln. It is crucially important that we are able to maintain both and I am grateful to the County Council for giving time for the Historic Lincoln Trust and the Usher Gallery Trust to try and find a solution that will ensure the survival of the Usher as one of the finest of our provincial art galleries and, with the collection of James Ward Usher, the greatest benefaction the city or county has ever received.

Please enjoy your visit and come back and bring your friends.

Patrick, Lord Cormack
Chairman, Historic Lincoln Trust

The Victoria and Albert Museum

The Victoria and Albert Museum, or V&A, is the world's leading Museum of Art, Design and Performance. Founded in 1852 to raise the standard of British design and make works of art available to all, our purpose is to champion creative industry, inspire the next generation of artists and innovators, and spark our visitors' imaginations.

Today, the V&A welcomes around four million visitors each year. We care for a world-class collection of over 2.7 million objects, spanning 5000 years, and house seventeen national collections showcasing objects of intricate craft and remarkable beauty. We also serve as a centre of excellence for innovative curatorship, conservation and research. We are a place for cutting-edge immersive exhibitions, scholarly displays and international festivals. We house a great number of unrivalled permanent galleries, and we continue to provide a natural home for art and design education in the United Kingdom.

The question of what, exactly, the V&A collects and displays is not always easy to define. Our first director, Henry Cole, described the museum in 1857 as 'a refuge for destitute collections'. More than a century later, then-director Sir Roy Strong called it 'an extremely capacious handbag'. The V&A's foundation as 'the central storehouse or treasury of Science and Art for the use of the whole Kingdom' has always given the museum a broad remit to collect objects from many periods, disciplines and regions, and has often allowed the museum to take on objects that do not easily fit into other national collections.

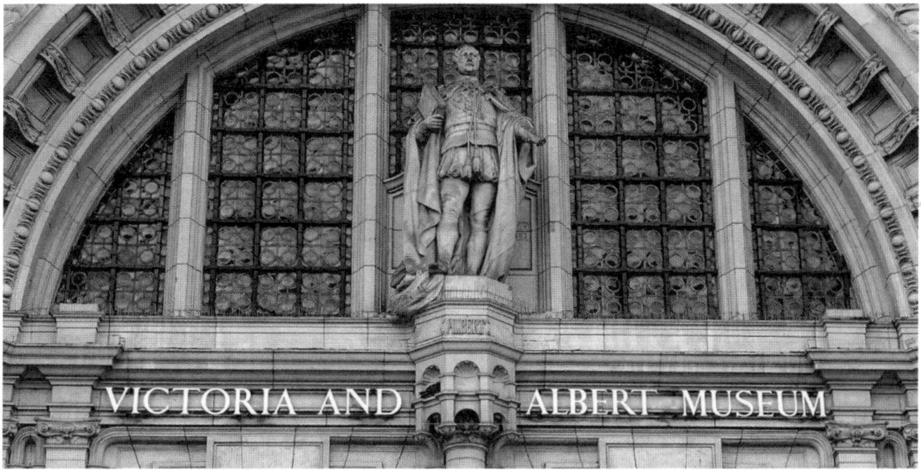

Since the very beginning, our objects have come from an eclectic range of sources. Some of the museum's earliest collections began with holdings from the East India Company. These formed the basis of the museum's South Asian collections, and 'Tipu's Tiger' - which can today be seen at the entrance to the South Asia galleries - remains one of the V&A's most intriguing and popular exhibits. The museum's impressive cast collection was the result of Henry Cole's 1867 'Convention for Promoting Universally Reproductions of Works of Art for the Benefit of Museums of All Countries', which aimed to gather examples of art and design from around the world into the galleries. Today the famous Cast Courts – which reopened in 2018 after an extensive ten-year refurbishment – are still some of the museum's iconic galleries, with their plaster casts of Trajan's Column, Michaelangelo's David and the Portico de la Gloria from Santiago de Compostela to name but a few. Along with the opening of our Photography Centre, these updated galleries have allowed us to tap into our founding principles and update them for today's audiences.

There is also a strong contemporary focus in our collecting, and we are committed to showcasing examples of the very best art and design being produced today. Our pioneering Rapid Response strategy collects objects as soon as they become newsworthy, allowing curators to respond immediately to contemporary issues and to collect pieces which may one day hold their own place in the history of design. Each new acquisition in this collection raises important questions about globalisation, popular culture, political and social change, demographics, technology or the law.

The V&A's founding mission – of bringing the designed world to new audiences in compelling ways – continues to resonate throughout our activities. It can be seen in our programme of exhibitions such as our recent blockbuster Christian Dior: Designer of Dreams and our current show Food: Bigger than the Plate; evening openings with our pioneering Friday Late events; digital expansion with our collections increasingly accessible online; and contemporary interventions such as London Design Festival, a week-long celebration of design.

Our educational mission also goes far beyond South Kensington. The opening of V&A Dundee in September has brought the V&A and its collections to new audiences in Tayside. An international centre of design, this new museum stands at the heart of the £1 billion transformation of the Dundee waterfront, once part of the city's docklands. Its galleries present the brilliance of Scottish creativity, as well as the best of design from around the world. Plans are also underway for the redevelopment of our Museum of Childhood, in Bethnal Green, which was constructed in 1872 using the original iron structure – the 'Brompton Boilers' – in which the South Kensington Museum was first housed. And in our work to reach the widest possible audience, V&A East - a new

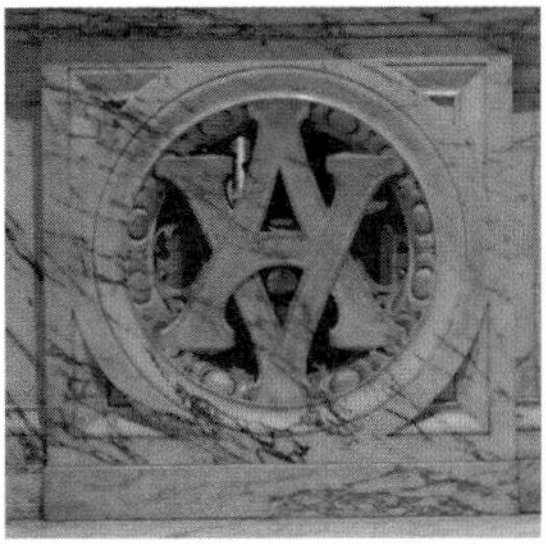

Stratford Waterfront museum, and a Collection and Research Centre in the Queen Elizabeth Olympic Park - is set to revolutionise how the V&A's world-leading collection can be accessed, explored and experienced. Opening in 2023, these two interconnected sites will share our collection in ways that have not been possible before.

We also continue to nurture and to deepen our connections across the country, through national partnerships and skill-sharing, and we are immensely proud that our loans programme lends more to UK partners than any other museum. Our DesignLab Nation series of loans and partnerships with regional museums – from Coventry to Sunderland – is part of our efforts to support the teaching of the Design and Technology curriculum around the country, in the face of a steep decline in the uptake of creative subjects that can only be described as a crisis in our schools. V&A Innovate is the latest addition to these efforts, providing resources to schools and teachers across England to support teaching at KS3 level. Now, more than ever, the V&A has a social and cultural imperative to creative education that still leads our purpose.

'Beauty, which is what is meant by art, using the word in its widest sense, is, I contend, no mere accident to human life, which people can take or leave as they choose, but a positive necessity of life'. These words were spoken by William Morris, who maintained a close relationship with the V&A during his lifetime. Morris's sentiments on the democratic importance of beauty is as important today as it was in his lifetime. And like Morris, we at the V&A 'do not want art for a few, any more than education for a few, or freedom for a few'.

The importance of museums in today's troubled national and global landscape seems more compelling than ever. Museums have a vital role to play in challenging chauvinism, celebrating cosmopolitanism, and serving as trustful intermediaries in an era of 'fake news'. If we can continue to marry the educational mettle of Henry Cole with the aesthetic and progressive ideals of William Morris, we will remain true to our founding purpose.

Dr Tristram Hunt
Director, Victoria and Albert Museum

Joseph Mallord William Turner (1775-1851)

Venice from the Guidecca

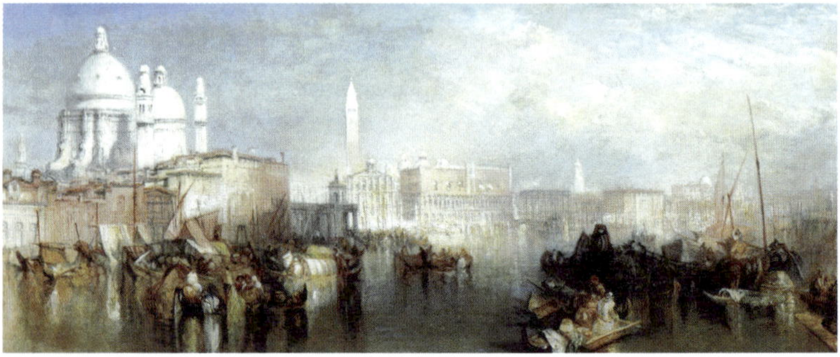

Oil on canvas, 1840. FA.208(O)

This view of Venice from the Guidecca Canal was commissioned by the collector John Sheepshanks and exhibited at the Royal Academy in 1840. In Turner's vision the city is romanticised, its ancient buildings bathed in Italian sunlight, contrasted with the bustling life on the water in the foreground. On the left rise the towers and domes of the church of Santa Maria della Salute, with the Doge's Palace beyond. At the time this was painted, Turner's style was out of favour with the critics and it was only the support of connoisseurs like Sheepshanks that enabled him to paint in his distinctive manner.

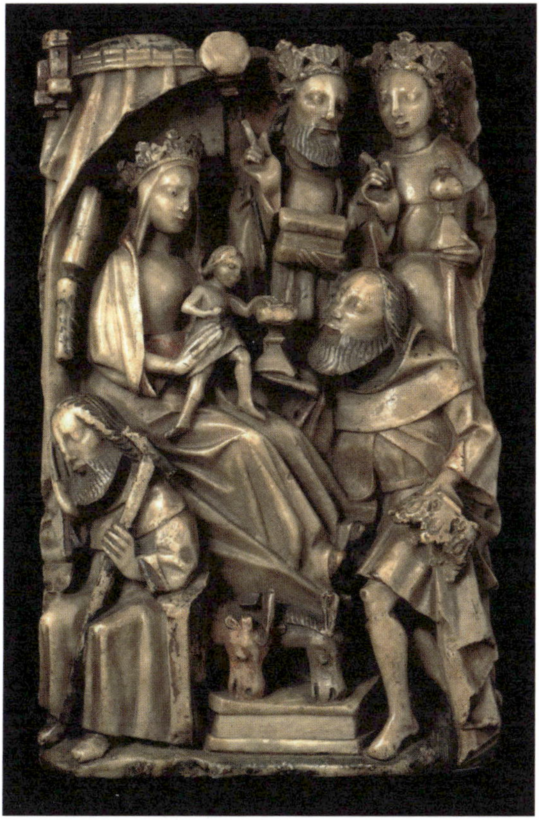

Carved and painted alabaster, 15th century. A.95-1946

Adoration of the Magi

This alabaster panel, produced in England during the second half of the fifteenth century, depicts the visit of the three Wise Men or Magi who travelled from the East to worship the Christ Child. In keeping with later tradition, the three men are here shown as kings. The Virgin Mary, who is crowned and wears a gown and a cloak, sits beneath a canopy with the Child on her lap. The Child is shown actively reaching out to touch the cup being offered to him by the kneeling king on the right. The other two kings stand behind, one with a box and the other with a second cup; they both point upwards towards a carved circle which no doubt originally bore a star. At the bottom left, Joseph is shown sleeping. Beneath the Virgin's feet can be seen the ox and the ass, feeding from the manger. Many of these English alabasters were made in Nottingham and the surrounding area.

The Young Victoria

On 6 November 1817 the young Princess Charlotte of Wales died, shortly after giving birth to a still-born son. This tragic event not only plunged the nation into mourning, it also created a succession crisis for the throne of the United Kingdom. Charlotte, had she lived, would eventually have ascended the throne as Queen, for the young Princess, as well as being the sole child and heir of her father, was remarkably the single legitimate grandchild of the ageing King George III.

George III and Queen Charlotte had produced a large family, of whom seven sons and four daughters were living in 1817. They did little to dispel widespread criticism that they were idle and extravagant pleasure-seekers. The King, in an attempt to stop his children making unsuitable marriages, secured the passing of the Royal Marriages Act of 1772, which required them to secure his permission before marrying. The unintended result was that several of the King's sons continued to live happily with their mistresses, the total number of their illegitimate children eventually exceeding fifty.

The need to produce an heir following the untimely death of Princess Charlotte appears to have animated the Royal Dukes, who seem to have hoped that whoever succeeded in thus perpetuating the Hanoverian lineage would be rewarded with a generous grant by Parliament. The two senior brothers were non-starters in what would come to be known as the 'baby race'. The Prince of Wales was estranged from his wife Caroline, whom he would later divorce amid spectacular controversy. The next brother, Frederick,

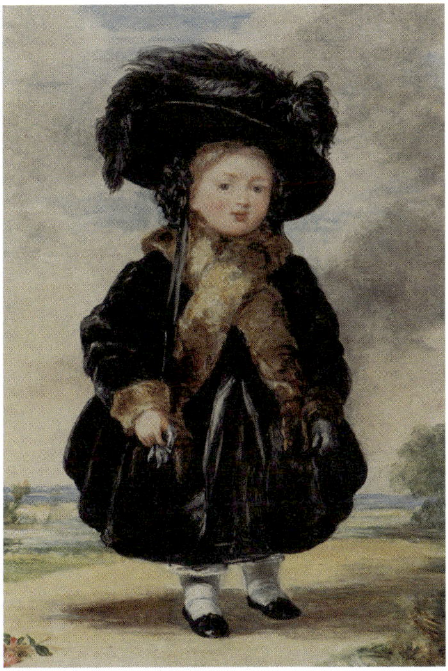

Stephen Poyntz Denning (1795-1864)

Princess Victoria, aged Four

This charming portrait shows the young Princess clad in a black pelisse, with a fox fur tippet crossed at her neck. On her head is a large black hat decorated with feathers. The sombre colours of her costume serve as a reminder that Victoria was a fatherless child, the Duke of Kent having died before she was a year old. The artist, Stephen Poyntz Denning, was Keeper of the Dulwich Picture Gallery from 1821 until his death in 1864. Starting life in humble circumstances, he became much admired as a portrait painter and miniaturist, exhibiting regularly at the Royal Academy.

Oil on panel, 1823.
DPG304

Duke of York, had married in 1791 Princess Frederica of Prussia; there were no children and the husband and wife had lived separately for many years. The Duke had served in the Army, not completely without distinction, and as commander-in-chief after 1798 introduced some necessary reforms, founding the Royal Military Academy at Woolwich. It is somewhat ironic that, in the words of the Complete Peerage, he 'is now chiefly remembered in the public mind as a man who marched his army up and down a hill'.

The favourites in the baby race were thus the two next senior Dukes, both as yet unmarried. The Duke of Clarence (the future King William IV) had spent much of his early life serving in the Royal Navy. While engaged in naval service, the young Prince spent the winter of 1781-2 in New York, at that time the last stronghold of English support in America. An audacious plan by rebel forces, camped in New Jersey on the opposite bank of the Hudson River, to capture the Prince in a surprise night attack was abandoned on being revealed prematurely. When the King's mental instability caused Prince William to be summoned back to England, he made several attempts to marry but none of his choices received the necessary approval of his father or his elder brother. Eventually he settled into an unofficial domestic bliss with Dorothy Bland, usually known as Mrs Jordan, a popular actress, with whom he had ten illegitimate children. By the time the 'baby race' began, however, he had already separated from his mistress, his need for a lawful marriage (and the Parliamentary grant that would result) being driven by his mounting debts. When the situation became urgent after the death of Princess Charlotte, his choice fell on Princess Adelaide of Saxe-Meiningen.

The next brother, Prince Edward (later Duke of Kent), was sent into the Army. As Colonel of the Royal Fusiliers, he gained a reputation as a severe disciplinarian. Stationed in Gibraltar in 1790, he entered upon his duties with enthusiasm, rising early every day to inspect and drill his troops and to order floggings for misdemeanours. Discontent among his soldiers rose to such a pitch that, back in London, the Government ordered him to proceed at once to North America, where it was hoped that his severity might be mitigated by the greater social opportunities that Canada would afford.

The first part of this plan had little effect; the Prince's zeal for discipline was unabated and his soldiers regarded him as a tyrant. Among the civilian population of Quebec, however, he became very popular. Such a society, with its French influences, would not look askance at the Prince taking a mistress, particularly one such as Madame Alphonsine de Montgenet de St Laurent. Madame de St Laurent remained as his 'wife' for nearly thirty years,

Sir Edwin Landseer (1802-1873)

Lion: A Newfoundland Dog

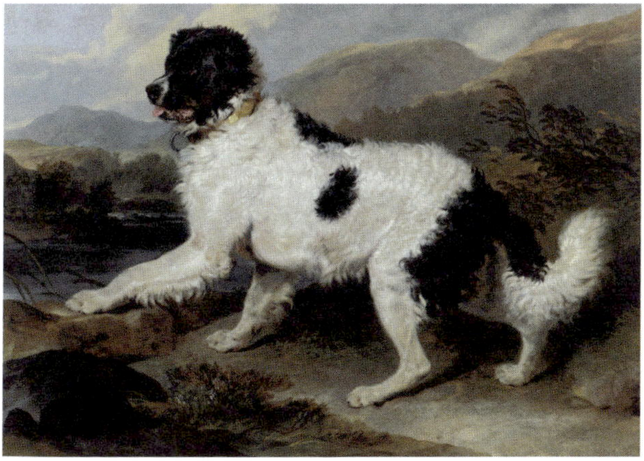

Oil on canvas, 1824.
852-1894

The young Landseer showed remarkable artistic gifts from an early age and his abilities were fostered and encouraged by his father, the Lincoln-born engraver John Landseer. At the age of fourteen, the boy entered the Royal Academy Schools where he was known affectionately by his master, Henry Fuseli, as 'my little dog boy', indicating that his talent for portraying animals was already notable. This painting of a Newfoundland dog was commissioned by its owner, W. H. de Merle; it is painted against a background derived from the scenery of the Scottish Highlands.

until the onset of the 'baby race' required the Prince (now Duke of Kent) to take a legitimate consort. One morning, shortly after the death of Princess Charlotte, the Duke and 'Madame' were sitting at breakfast, he opening his letters, she reading the newspaper. Suddenly she gave 'a gasp and a gurgle' and pointed in agitation to the paper where it was reported that 'it had become essential for the succession that the Duke of Kent should marry'.

So it was that, on 11 July 1818 (Madame de St Laurent having retired discreetly to a nunnery) an extraordinary double wedding took place at the royal palace of Kew. In the presence of Queen Charlotte and of the Prince Regent, the Archbishop of Canterbury officiated at the marriages of William, Duke of Clarence, to Adelaide, Princess of Saxe-Meiningen, and of Edward, Duke of Kent, to Victoire, Dowager Princess of Leiningen and sister of Prince Leopold of Saxe-Coburg, widower of the lamented Princess Charlotte.

Although the Duke of Clarence had produced several illegitimate offspring with Mrs Jordan, his attempts to produce a lawful heir were not successful. A daughter was born and died in March 1819 and a second girl, born in December 1820, lived less than three months. Meanwhile, the only child of the Duke and Duchess of Kent was born at Kensington Palace on 24 May 1819. The Prince Regent was annoyed to think that this little girl might supplant his own, as yet unborn, descendants, on the throne. At her christening, he was asked to choose her name. He chose 'Alexandrina' as a compliment to the Tsar of Russia and also as a name that would not suggest her as a future Queen. When it was suggested that one name was insufficient, he grumbled 'Then give her the mother's name as well'. In this unexpected way, the young Princess acquired the name that would come to be applied to a whole era – Victoria.

William Mulready (1786-1863)

First Love

Mulready was born in Ireland but his family moved to London while he was still a child. His precocious talent earned him a place at the Royal Academy Schools. After 1815 he concentrated on narrative and domestic subjects in which he achieved considerable success. 'First Love' is another painting from the Sheepshanks Collection. It depicts a young woman holding a baby as a young man looks on. In the background a woman raises a hand in greeting while a small boy with his hands raised runs towards the young couple. Two dogs play in the foreground. The artist leaves the ambiguity unresolved: is the 'First Love' of the title that of the young man for the girl or that of the girl for her child?

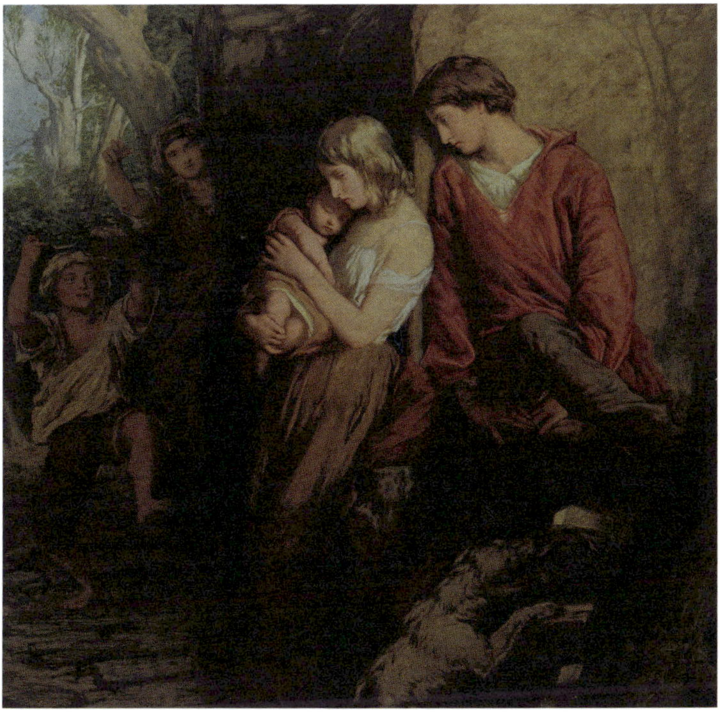

Oil on canvas,
1838-9
FA.141(O)

The Young Albert

The future Prince Consort was born on 26 August 1819 at Rosenau, the summer residence of the dukes of Saxe-Coburg-Saalfeld, situated about four miles from Coburg on the edge of the forest of Thuringen. He was the younger of the two sons of Duke Ernest and his wife, the former Princess Louise of Saxe-Gotha Altenburg. The Duke was a licentious philanderer and his unhappy wife took refuge in flirtations with other young men. This behaviour led in 1824 to her banishment from Coburg and her two sons; subsequently divorced, she died in 1831. The excesses of his father and the separation from his mother were to play a significant role in the development of Albert's character.

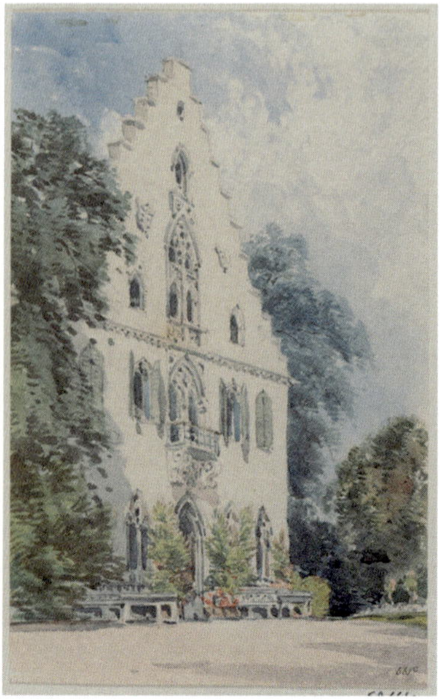

William Callow (1812-1908)

Sketch of the Schloss Rosenau at Coburg

Rosenau was the birthplace and childhood home of Albert of Saxe-Coburg, the future husband of Queen Victoria. This is one of a set of five sketches entitled 'Souvenirs of Rosenau'.

Paper: watercolour drawing, 1863.
PDP FA.661C

The young boy grew up at Rosenau under the supervision of a tutor. His lessons included mathematics, philosophy, geography and Latin. He adored his childhood home, surrounded by the natural world and the rhythmic pattern of rural life. Another great love was music. He studied with the local church organist and learned the rudiments of composition.

Keeping a close watch on his progress was his uncle Leopold, formerly the husband of the lamented Princess Charlotte of Wales and now, since 1831, King of the newly created state of Belgium. Leopold was also the uncle of the young Princess Victoria of Great Britain and it was he who provided the crucial link between the two cousins. In 1836 he arranged that Duke Ernest and his two sons should visit England. The elder of the two boys, Ernest, was destined to succeed his father; it was Albert that Leopold had chosen to be the future husband of Victoria. Although the seventeen-year-old Victoria found her cousin 'extremely good-looking', she had as yet no plans to marry. Her accession to the throne in the following year brought her a new and exciting role as Queen, as well as freeing her from the tutelage of her mother and Sir John Conroy. Albert had to wait, and he came to recognise the precarious nature of his position. As the younger son, he would inherit neither title nor estates and almost the only possible career path was a royal or an aristocratic marriage. If Victoria kept him waiting for years and then, after all, accepted someone else, his prospects might be bleak.

The young Queen's desire for independence, however, was soon compromised. Two crises in 1839 had shaken her confidence. Victoria's treatment of Lady Flora Hastings, one of her ladies-in-waiting, whom she had believed (without foundation) to be pregnant when she was in fact dying of cancer, had caused widespread gossip and scandal. Then her clash with Sir Robert Peel, the incoming Prime Minister, over the replacement of her Ladies of the Bedchamber led her to sail very close to the wind on a constitutional issue. Although she emerged victorious, keeping not only her Ladies but also her much loved Prime Minister, Lord Melbourne, she evidently had her inner doubts, admitting sixty years later, 'Yes! It was a mistake.' Another difficulty involved her mother, who had intrigued against Victoria during the affair of Lady Flora Hastings. It was impossible to live with her but, under the social norms of the time, impossible to live without her so long as the Queen was unmarried. Victoria was coming to realise that in her exalted position she needed someone close at hand on whose advice and support she could rely.

Outwardly the Queen was still declaring that she was not ready to marry just yet. She wrote to her uncle King Leopold, asking that a proposed visit from her cousins Albert and Ernest be called off and insisting that the King make it clear to her what he had done in encouraging Albert to hope for an 'engagement'. Diplomatically, Leopold sidestepped any mention of his niece's feelings about Albert, saying merely that the visit must go ahead as planned. Albert, after all, had agreed to wait on condition that Victoria would marry him in the end. The Queen, advised by Lord Melbourne, agreed that it would be unfair to keep Albert 'dangling'. Surely there would be no harm in the cousins just meeting?

On 10 October 1839, a day Victoria would remember for the rest of her life, Albert and his brother, exhausted from a rough Channel crossing and without their baggage which had been mislaid, arrived at Windsor. The Queen stood at the head of the great staircase to greet them. Albert was tense and nervous, knowing that he must give Victoria an ultimatum and expecting to be rebuffed. Still wearing the clothes in which he had travelled, he began with his brother to climb the stone stairs. Yet as the Queen looked down on him, she was smitten: 'It was with some emotion that I beheld Albert – who is beautiful.'

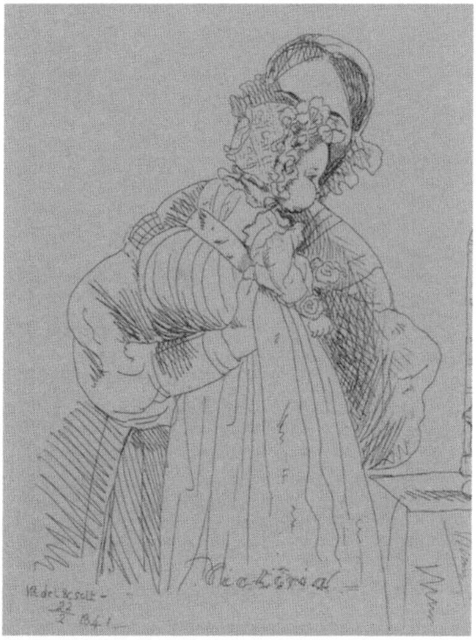

Etching, 1841
E.2175-1932

Queen Victoria (1819-1901)

Victoria, Princess Royal, later Empress Frederick of Germany, as a baby in the arms of a nurse.

In 1840, while the Queen was expecting her first child, she and Albert set up an etching press at Buckingham Palace. Victoria recorded in her Journal: 'We spent a delightful, peaceful morning – singing after breakfast, and etching together'. After the birth of her daughter 'Vicky', she continued to etch and her skill in the use of this medium increased. She noted that 'the three sketches of Victoria were done at once on to the plate'.

Everything changed in that moment. The young Queen, who until then had wanted to postpone any marriage, now could hardly wait for her wedding. Five days later she sent for Albert to meet her in her favourite Blue Closet, where she proposed to him, telling him 'that it would make me too happy if he would consent to what I wished'. The four months preceding the wedding were notable for some unseemly wrangling in Parliament about Albert's rank, status and income. A proposed annual grant of £50,000 (the same amount granted to Leopold as husband of Princess Charlotte) was reduced to £30,000 by an amendment successfully proposed by the irascible Colonel Charles Sibthorp, MP for Lincoln (an action that the Queen did not forget).

The wedding ceremony took place on 10 February 1840 in the Chapel Royal of St James's Palace. The Queen wore a white satin dress trimmed with Honiton lace, a diamond necklace, a sapphire brooch given by her Albert, and a wreath of orange blossom. At the Chapel she was joined by twelve train-bearers clad in white dresses which Victoria had sketched herself. The ceremony was conducted by the Archbishop of Canterbury, William Howley. Later, after a wedding breakfast at Buckingham Palace, they departed for a honeymoon at Windsor.

There is no doubting the deep mutual love and affection between Victoria and Albert. It is true that there were fundamental differences in temperament between the pair. Albert's nature was disciplined and even prudish, a reaction to the licentiousness of his father and his elder brother, while Victoria loved eating and drinking, dancing, society and late nights. Initially Albert was also frustrated by his subordinate position in the Royal Household, complaining to a schoolfriend, 'I am only the husband, and not the master in the house'. While the Queen dealt with state papers, her husband's role was at first peripheral ('Albert helped me with the blotting paper when I signed'). But Victoria's frequent pregnancies (between 1840 and 1857 the couple had nine children) left her increasingly dependent on her husband's help in dealing with public affairs and she came to rely more and more on Albert as her Private Secretary. That they succeeded in finding how to work through their difficulties is clear both from the extensive record of their shared life and from the Queen's overwhelming grief on Albert's death. As one of Albert's biographers has concluded, their marriage, 'arranged as it was, and stormy as at times it could be, remains one of the greatest love stories outside fiction'.

Sir Edwin Landseer (1802-1873)

A Highland Breakfast

Landseer first visited Scotland in 1824 and the landscape and scenery, especially of the Highlands, had a profound effect on him. This painting, exhibited at the Royal Academy in 1834, was one of a sequence of Highland subjects which he painted at the time. It depicts a young mother breastfeeding her baby while a group of dogs enjoy their own breakfast at a nearby tub. The work was acquired by the collector John Sheepshanks and formed part of his gift to the South Kensington Museum in 1857.

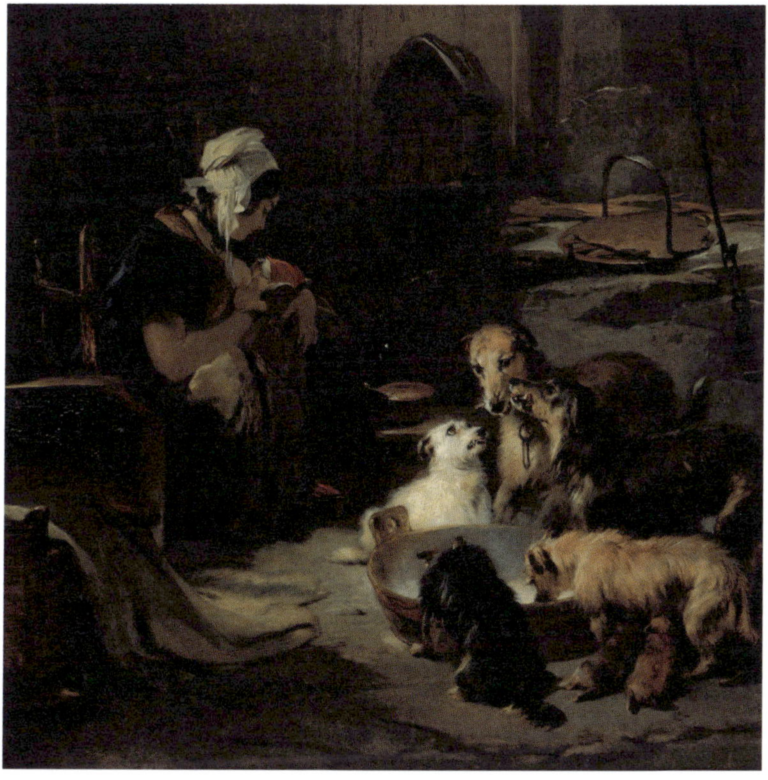

Oil on panel, c.1834. FA.87(O)

Henry Cole

Born in 1808, Henry Cole was the son of an army officer. He was educated at Christ's Hospital School. As his parents could not afford to send him to university, he started work as a clerk in the Record Commission, apparently securing the post because of his neat handwriting. From 1826, Cole's family rented lodgings in a house belonging to the novelist, Thomas Love Peacock, who encouraged him to try his hand at journalism and introduced him to a circle of 'philosophical radicals', notably John Stuart Mill. Through such men he became a believer in utilitarianism, Jeremy Bentham's philosophy of 'the greatest happiness of the greatest number'.

Such views led Cole to write articles for the press exposing what he saw as corruption within the Record Commission, as a result of which he was dismissed. A subsequent parliamentary inquiry vindicated him however and he was reinstated as a senior assistant keeper in the new Public Record Office. His interests and enthusiasms went well beyond his archival duties and he found time to assist Rowland Hill in the introduction of the penny post in 1840. This radical change in mass communication no doubt influenced his publication of the first Christmas card three years later.

During the 1840s, Cole also became involved in the politics of the expanding railway network, campaigning for a uniform narrow gauge. He also turned his attention to artistic ventures, writing a guidebook to Westminster Abbey, publishing children's books under the nom de plume of Felix Summerly and in 1846 winning a silver medal in a competition sponsored by the Society of Arts to produce designs for a new tea service.

Sir Henry Cole (1808-1882)

Tea Service

In 1845 the Society of Arts offered a prize for a new design for a tea service. Henry Cole, who was campaigning to improve British design, submitted this entry which won a silver medal in the competition. Cole's success encouraged him to found 'Felix Summerly's Art Manufactures' and he persuaded his friend Herbert Minton to produce the tea service at his factory in Stoke-on-Trent. The 'Felix Summerly' enterprise was short-lived, as Cole's energies were increasingly absorbed by the Great Exhibition of 1851. However, the separate parts of his tea service remained in production for some time; the cup in particular became a Minton standard and continued to be made into the twentieth century. This tea set was formerly displayed in the Museum of Practical Geology in Jermyn Street, a subsidiary of the South Kensington Museum. It was transferred to the V&A in 1901.

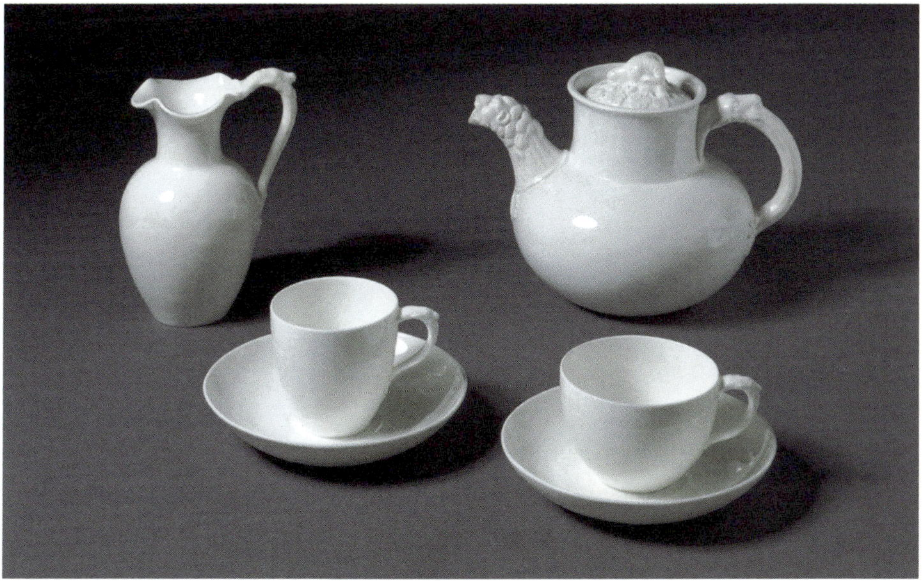

Earthenware. 2741&A-1901

John Callcott Horsley (1817-1903)

Christmas Card

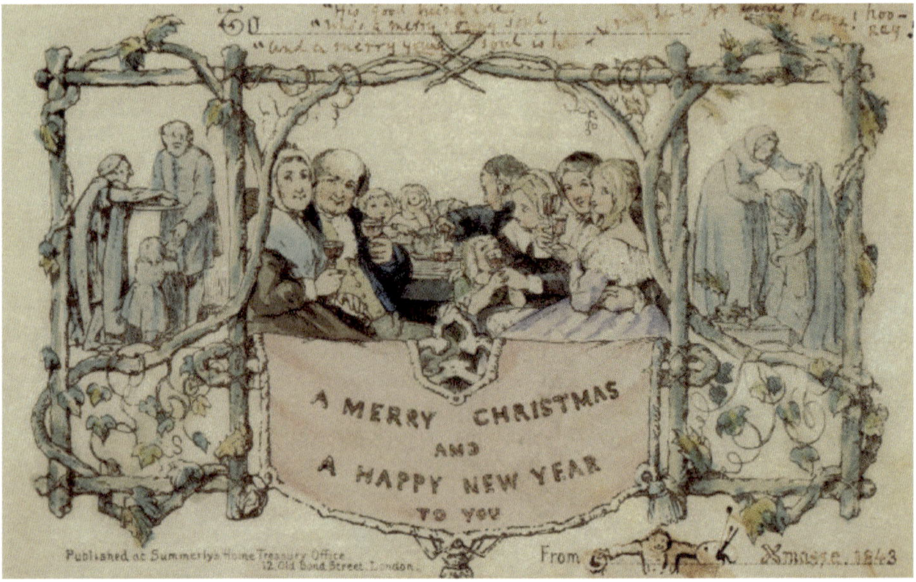

Hand-coloured lithograph on card, 1843.
MSL/1987/3293

Widely acknowledged as the first Christmas card, this was designed by John Callcott Horsley (1817-1903) for Henry Cole, subsequently the first Director of the South Kensington Museum. Cole's energy and enthusiasm took him far beyond his official position as Senior Assistant Keeper at the Public Record Office. His involvement with Rowland Hill over the introduction of the penny post in 1840 led him to devise a means of sending seasonal greetings at Christmas time. Horsley's design shows the extended Cole family in the centre, raising a Christmas toast to their friends, while the two outer panels illustrate seasonal acts of charity. This example was evidently sent to Cole by Horsley himself, who sketched a self-portrait at the foot of the card in place of a signature; he holds his palette and brushes in one hand and doffs his hat with the other 33.

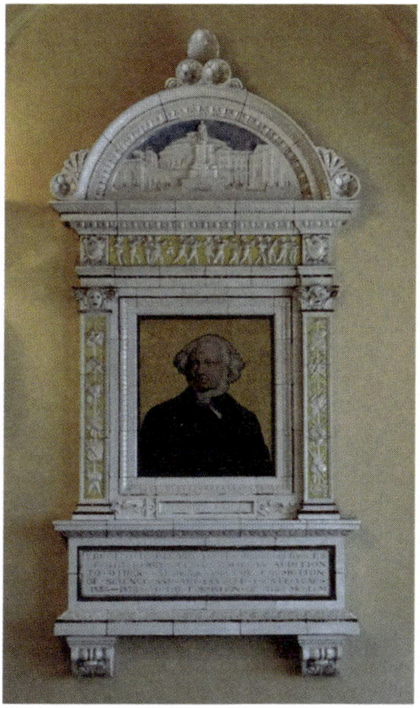

(Henry Cole: mosaic on the first landing of the Ceramic Staircase at the Victoria and Albert Museum. The portrait was made by Cole's niece, Florence Cole, at the South Kensington Museum Mosaic Class. The relief above the portrait depicts the buildings of 'Albertopolis', including the Albert Hall.)

Cole's involvement with the Society of Arts led to a series of exhibitions of modern manufactures intended to promote good design. This was not enough to satisfy him, however, and he persuaded Prince Albert, the Society's President, to join in promoting an international exhibition of manufacture and design which came to fruition as the Great Exhibition of 1851. Cole played a central part in the success of the Exhibition, energetically promoting the idea in its early stages and then undertaking the considerable task of getting all the exhibits together in the Crystal Palace.

Afterwards, Cole was closely involved with the realisation of Albert's dream of a museum and educational quarter in what was known as 'Albertopolis', overseeing the creation of the South Kensington Museum (which later developed into the Victoria and Albert and the Science Museums), the gardens of the Royal Horticultural Society, the second Great Exhibition of 1862 and the building of the Albert Hall. In turns passionate, abrasive and authoritarian, he was not always easy to work with, but his achievement was both impressive and lasting. He retired in 1873, was knighted two years later, dying in 1882.

The Great Exhibition of 1851

The first decade of the royal marriage has been characterised as the 'hungry forties', a period of great economic hardship and suffering among the poor. The Chartists campaigned for further parliamentary reform; others agitated against the corn laws which supported landowners but kept the price of bread high. Meanwhile in Ireland, unimaginable numbers died in the Potato Famine. Prince Albert was particularly concerned that more should be done to ameliorate what was known as 'the condition of England question'. In particular he sought to promote improvements in education, the provision of social housing and the spread of good design and technology as a means of furthering British commerce.

It was at this point that the Society of Arts, of which Albert was President, came up with a proposal for a major exhibition in London to showcase British manufacturing. The inspiration behind the idea was Henry Cole, whose official job was as an assistant keeper in the Public Record Office but who had also been instrumental in the introduction of the penny post (1840) and the invention of the first Christmas card (1843). At a time when free trade was expanding markets globally, the potential boost to the economy to be derived from such an exhibition was encouraging.

Cole went on a speaking tour of the country to arouse enthusiasm for the Exhibition, while Albert arranged for the appointment of a Royal Commission to oversee the project. A site was chosen in Hyde Park and plans were put forward for a large 'cathedral style' building to house the display. The proposed building, though designed largely by Isambard Kingdom Brunel, was not well received, being likened to an engine shed with an outsize dome. One of the

Henry Courtenay Selous (1803-1890)

The Opening of the Great Exhibition on 1 May 1851

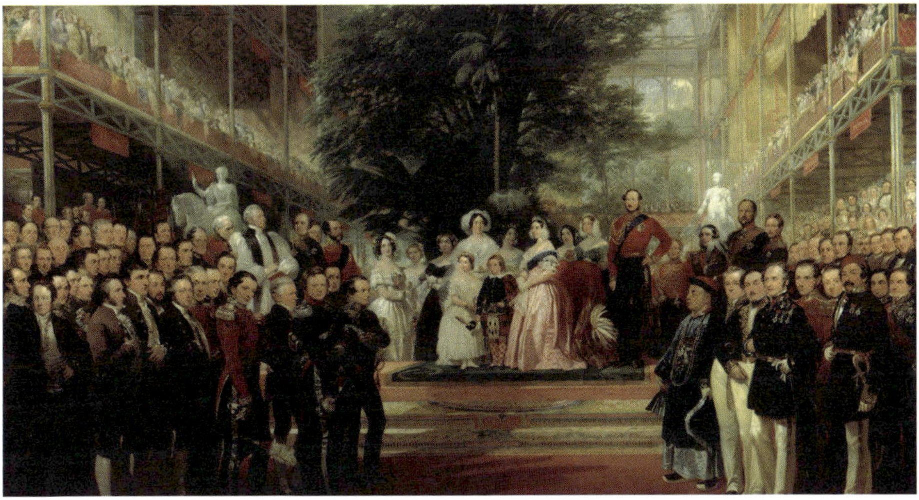

Oil on canvas, 1851-2.
329-1889

The Queen drove to the Crystal Palace in the State Coach, accompanied by Prince Albert and their two eldest children, Vickie and Bertie. The royal party processed up the central aisle, surrounded by thousand of season-ticket holders, to a special dais facing the central fountain; one of Hyde Park's elm trees can be seen behind. Selous's painting of the scene shows the Archbishop of Canterbury, to the left of the royal party, asking God's blessing on the Exhibition. Among the foreign diplomats in the foreground is the 'Chinese Mandarin' who was so moved by the singing of Handel's Hallelujah Chorus that he approached the Queen to make his obeisance. In fact, he was not a diplomat at all but the skipper of a Chinese junk on the Thames who had been swept into the procession by accident. Commemorative paintings of events such as this were often produced in the Victorian period; the sale of prints made subsequently could provide a substantial income for the artist.

most prominent critics was the irascible Colonel Charles Sibthorp, Member of Parliament for Lincoln. He waded in against the proposed Exhibition, seeing it as an attack on the morale of all true Englishmen. 'An exhibition of the industry of all nations, forsooth! An exhibition of the trumpery and trash of foreign countries, to the detriment of our own already too much oppressed manufacturers.'

The proposed building continued to attract criticism. It would be a monstrosity, it would be hideously expensive and would remain for ever as a blot on the landscape of the Park (where it would also involve cutting down some of the trees). Now Albert produced his masterstroke. He and the Queen had stayed with the Duke of Devonshire at Chatsworth and had admired the Duke's magnificent new greenhouses, built by Joseph Paxton. Paxton was encouraged to submit plans for the exhibition hall and the result was the famous 'Crystal Palace', a masterpiece in iron and glass, built entirely from prefabricated parts and designed and constructed in less than eight months.

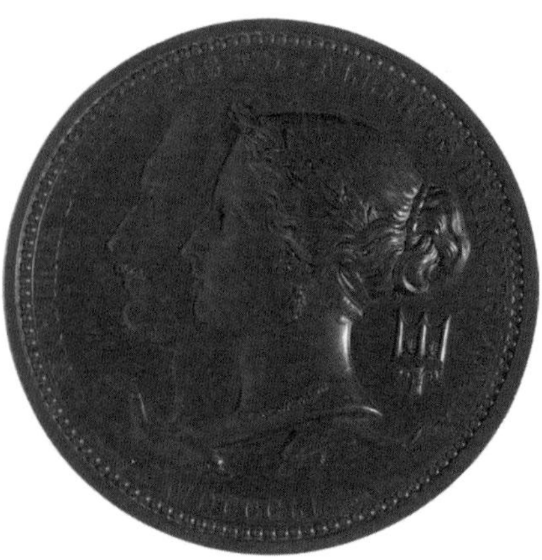

William Wyon *(1795-1851),*
designer and maker

Leonard Charles Wyon *(1826-1891),*
designer and maker

Medal: Prize medal for the Great Exhibition of 1851, depicting Queen Victoria and Prince Albert. The Prize Medal was awarded to more than 2,900 exhibitors at the Exhibition. This example is inscribed to the School of Design.
Struck bronze: London, 1851.
National Art Library: 38041800799207

The building was so large that it was high enough to enclose a number of elm trees within its structure. Although this satisfied the critics, it was said to have led to an unforeseen difficulty which distressed Albert as the grand opening approached. It appeared that sparrows nesting in the trees were causing a mess which made it impossible to display valuable exhibits. The Queen sent for the Prime Minister, Lord John Russell who suggested that the Guards be sent in to shoot the birds. Albert pointed out that this would result in the destruction of the building. Russell then suggested that they consult the Foreign Secretary, Lord Palmerston, who recommended spreading bird lime on the branches of the trees. Albert replied that this would not work either, because the sparrows were now roosting on the structure of the building itself. The two statesmen, at a loss, now advised the Queen to send for the Duke of Wellington. The Iron Duke arrived and the Queen explained the difficulty. He spoke two words: "Sparrowhawks, Ma'am".

The Great Exhibition was opened, on schedule, on 1 May 1851. The Queen, dressed in pink and silver, wearing the ribbon of the Garter and the Koh-i-Noor diamond, drove to the Crystal Palace in an open carriage. The Times compared the event to the concourse of all peoples on the Day of Judgment, and the religious aspect of the Exhibition was summed up in the words printed at the head of the catalogue: The Earth is the Lord's and all that therein is. (The evangelical Lord Ashley complained about the use of the Prayer Book version of the Psalm.) The Queen remembered afterwards 'The tremendous cheering, the joy expressed in every face, the vastness of the building … and my beloved husband the creator of this great Peace Festival'.

J. Michael

Part of the Fine Arts Court, 1851

This watercolour was one of a series of views of the Great Exhibition, reproduced in a contemporary guide which was published as a souvenir of the event. The Crystal Palace was likened to a great cathedral and the Fine Arts Court was situated on the north side of the 'Nave', close to the two transepts. In the centre can be seen an exuberant Gothic Revival font, probably made by J. Castle of Oxford.

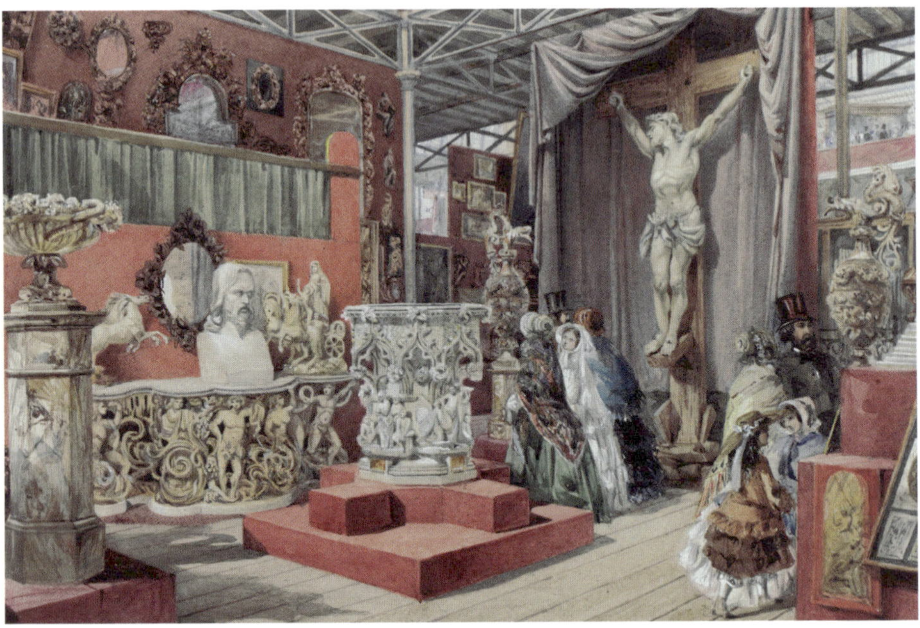

Watercolour drawing, 1851.
E.8-2007.

The success of the Exhibition exceeded all expectations and silenced its critics. The Queen herself visited almost every day until she left London for Osborne at the end of July. Over six million people went to the Crystal Palace to see the items on display – over 100,000 of them – including not only British manufactures and works of art but also American machinery, German glassware, Belgian furniture, Russian cloth and Persian tapestries. There were examples of machinery, a model of the Liverpool docks, textiles, clocks and watches, precious metals and jewellery, glass and ceramics, furniture. As Tennyson wrote in his 'Exhibition Ode', 'All of beauty, all of use / That one fair planet can produce'.

The Great Exhibition of 1851 also ended up in profit. When the income and expenditure were calculated afterwards, there proved to be a surplus of £213,305 15s 8d. Financial success was due in large part to the 'shilling visitors', of whom there were 4.4 million, their entrance fees adding up to £220,000. The surplus was used to establish an estate of educational and cultural organisations in South Kensington to be known, after its great progenitor, as 'Albertopolis', and still flourishing today in the form of much-loved institutions such as the Albert Hall, the Science Museum, the Natural History Museum and the Victoria and Albert Museum.

William Mulready (1786-1863)

The Fight Interrupted

Exhibited at the Royal Academy in 1816, this painting is a fine example of Mulready's narrative style. He depicts a school playground, in which the black-gowned Master has intervened to stop a fight – but the boy he has seized by the ear is the wrong culprit. As a boy, Mulready had himself been encouraged to learn the art of boxing; he was given lessons by the famous pugilist Mendoza. Indeed, it was said that Mulready's first meeting with his patron, John Sheepshanks, took place when the painter used his boxing skills to defend Sheepshanks from an assailant. This painting formed part of the Sheepshanks gift to the South Kensington Museum in 1857.

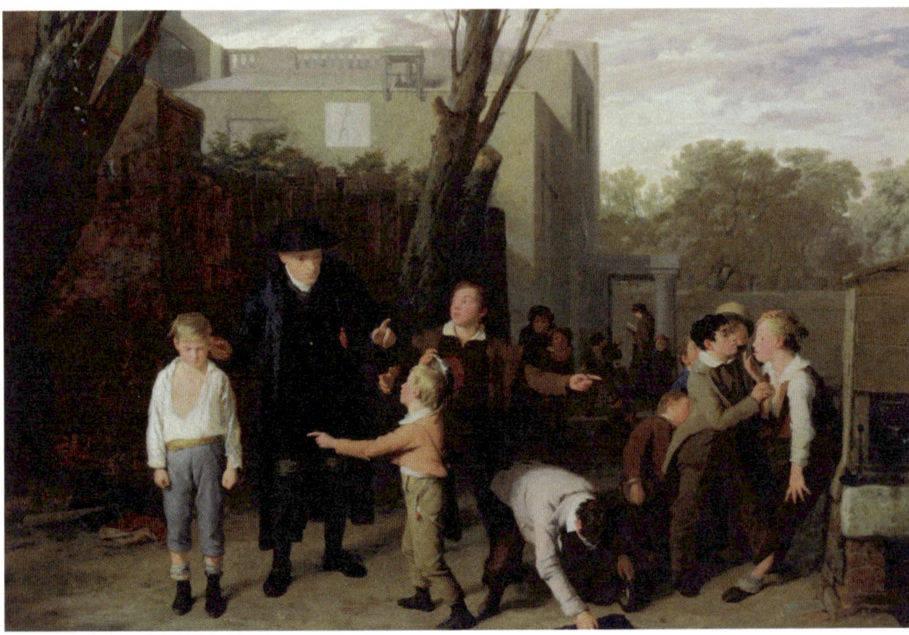

Oil on panel, 1816.
FA.139(O)

John Sheepshanks & his 'National Gallery of British Art'

John Sheepshanks (1787-1863) was the son of a wealthy cloth manufacturer from Leeds who retired from the family business at 40 and moved to London to indulge his passion for collecting art. He began collecting copies of old master paintings but when the National Gallery opened in Trafalgar Square in 1824, he realised that there was little he could contribute to that field. Instead, he turned his attention to contemporary British art, collecting works by the likes of J. M. W. Turner, John Constable, Sir Edwin Landseer and William Mulready. He employed the artist Richard Redgrave as his curator. He developed good relationships with many artists and commissioned works directly from them, as well as adding to his collection at the saleroom and the summer exhibitions at the Royal Academy. He particularly admired the work of Mulready who painted Sheepshanks in his London home. He eventually owned 30 paintings by the artist and the two became close friends.

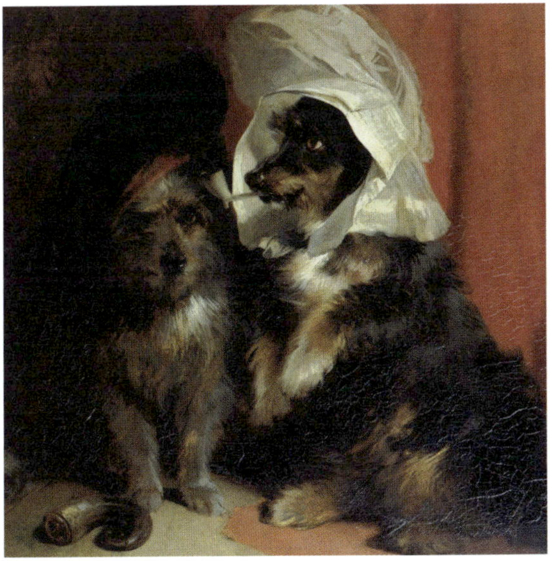

Sir Edwin Landseer *(1802 -1873)*
Comical Dogs

Sheepshanks started to think about giving his collection to the nation in 1852. When the Museum of Manufacturers moved to South Kensington and with Redgrave responsible for national art education and all new acquisitions, Sheepshanks saw the opportunity to offer his collection to the museum to form the basis of a national gallery of British art. He gave 233 paintings and 298 watercolours and drawings to the museum. The terms of his donation required a permanent gallery to display his collection and so on 25 November 1856, the museum's engineer-architect Captain Francis Fowke set to work on building the first permanent gallery on the South Kensington site.

Just a few months later on 20 June 1857, Queen Victoria, accompanied by her husband Prince Albert, opened the South Kensington Museum. They visited the newly constructed gallery and marvelled at the celebration of contemporary British art within. The Royal Couple admired many of the same artists including Victoria's favourite painter Landseer. That evening she noted the occasion in her diary: 'It was very interesting, & the Museum extremely well arranged. We also saw the Sheepshanks collection of pictures.'

Sheepshanks hoped that his gift of paintings would encourage other collectors to give works of art to the museum for the enjoyment and education of all. Indeed, in the next few years the museum benefitted from the generosity of several important collectors including Richard Ellison, MP for Lincoln from 1796 to 1812, whose gift of works on paper firmly established the museum's watercolours as that national collection.

Sheepshanks strongly believed in the importance of making art accessible to all, very much in keeping with Prince Albert's vision to make the museum 'a schoolroom for everyone'. In the conditions of his gift, he stipulated that the museum must increase its opening hours to include weekday evenings and Sundays so that workers 'who are actively employed in the day might have the means of visiting the galleries and enjoying the pictures in these their only leisure hours'. The museum was the first in the world to be gas lit, a convenience led by Cole who hoped that this would not only bring in more visitors after work but would 'furnish a powerful antidote to the gin palace'.

The paintings in this exhibition offer a window into Sheepshanks' personal taste and shed light on the 19th-century contemporary art world. He was particularly fond of literary subjects, small genre scenes, landscapes and paintings of animals. Thanks to Sheepshanks' and Redgrave's meticulous care of the collection, these are some of the best preserved examples of paintings from the early nineteenth century anywhere. While their vision for a national gallery of British art was eventually supplanted by the opening of the Tate Gallery in 1897, the collection remains a significant part of the V&A's holdings and gives us access to the personalities and ambitions of the key figures who spearheaded the early growth the museum.

Emily Knight
Assistant Curator of Paintings, Victoria and Albert Museum

J. C. Lanchenick

South Kensington Museum: South End of Iron Building

The original structure of the South Kensington Museum, completed in 1857, was officially known as 'The Iron Museum'. After an original design by the architect Gottfried Semper had been rejected by Parliament as too expensive, Prince Albert suggested a quicker and cheaper alternative, in view of the pressing need to move the collections from Marlborough House to more spacious premises. A company which specialised in providing prefabricated corrugated iron barracks and hospitals for the colonies supplied three buildings which were linked together to form the Museum. The result was described by one critic as 'a huge lugubrious hospital for decayed railway carriages', while The Builder likened it to three steam boilers lying on their sides, resulting in the nickname 'The Brompton Boilers'. The temporary structure continued to house much of the South Kensington Museum until 1865 when it was dismantled and moved to Bethnal Green. It now forms part of the V&A Museum of Childhood).

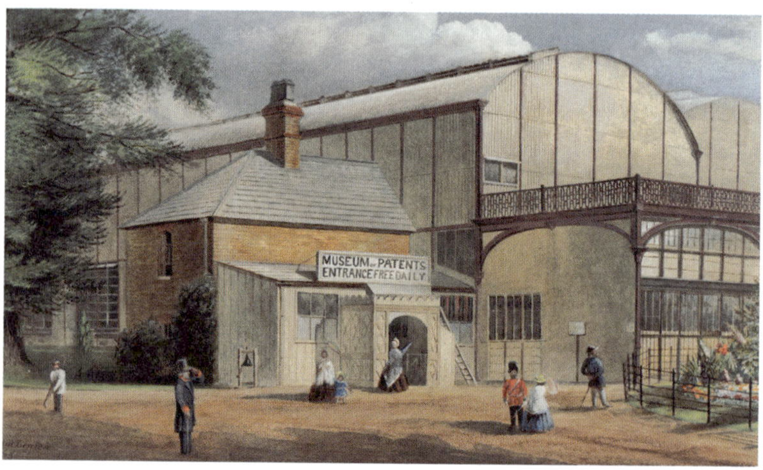

Watercolour, 1863.
PDP 2816.

Furnishing fabric: floral chintz

Made in Lancashire about 1850, this highly floral fabric was displayed in Henry Cole's controversial exhibition, 'False Principles in Design', which he put on in 1852 at the Museum of Ornamental Art in Marlborough House. Cole had seen the fundamental purpose of the Great Exhibition as the education of the community in Art, and 'False Principles' was intended to show the very worst examples of design. This fabric, which still bears traces of its exhibition label, was condemned for the 'direct imitation of nature'; it was felt that these branches of lilac and rose trees should not be contorted to fit the shape of chairs and cushions. There is little evidence that these strictures had any effect on public taste and chintz continued to be very popular; Queen Victoria herself used it in the decoration of Osborne House.

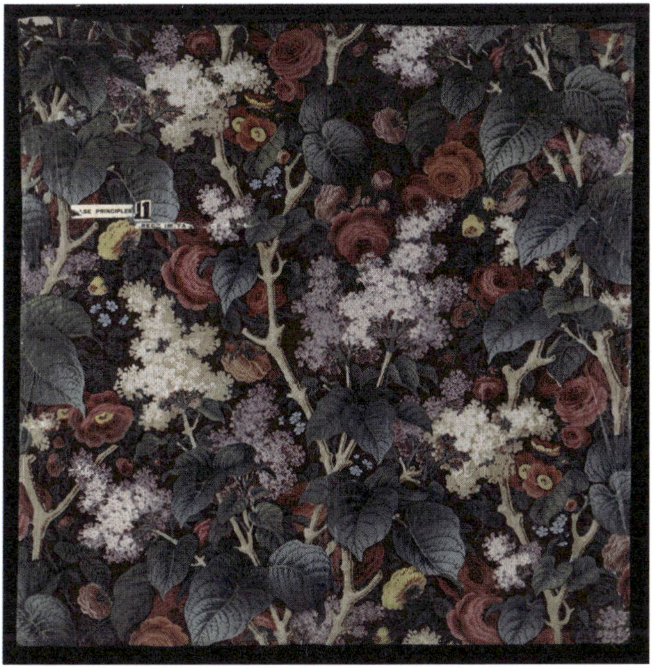

Furnishing fabric, chintz, highly floral: Lancashire, c.1850. T.10-1933.

From Brompton Park House to the V&A

Prince Albert was keen to build on the success of the Great Exhibition of 1851. Under his guidance, the Exhibition Commission bought up the various parcels of land in Brompton which would eventually form the estate on which 'Albertopolis', the new museums complex, would develop. The Government made a grant of £5,000 and a 'buying committee', whose members included Henry Cole and A. W. N. Pugin, was appointed to purchase exhibits from the Crystal Palace. In total, 244 exhibits were acquired, including a considerable number from India.

In 1852 Cole was appointed Secretary of the Government School of Design. He undoubtedly owed this appointment to the support of Prince Albert who had in October 1851 written to thank him for his tireless work for the Great Exhibition. The School of Design had opened in 1837 with the aim of disseminating knowledge of Fine Arts, particularly to manufacturers. Located in Somerset House on The Strand, the School had for some time nursed the ambition to create a museum of 'specimens of tasteful manufacture'. Although this ambition remained unfulfilled, a considerable collection of 'teaching objects' had been assembled for the benefit of the students. Many of the items were plaster casts but in 1843 the School acquired a set of lunettes and pilasters copied from Raphael's decoration of the Loggia at the Vatican. A report published in the same year noted, intriguingly, the acquisition of 'Gothic enrichments from Lincoln Cathedral'.

William Linnaeus Casey (1835-1870)

Marlborough House: Second Room

This watercolour provides a record of one of the exhibition rooms in the Museum of Ornamental Manufactures at Marlborough House. Prominently displayed are items of Renaissance maiolica from the Soulages Collection, acquired for the Museum on loan in 1856. The Prime Minister, Lord Palmerston, was not impressed, saying 'What is the use of such rubbish to our manufacturers?' and he refused to buy the collection for the nation. Subsequently Henry Cole succeeded in purchasing the collection in instalments.

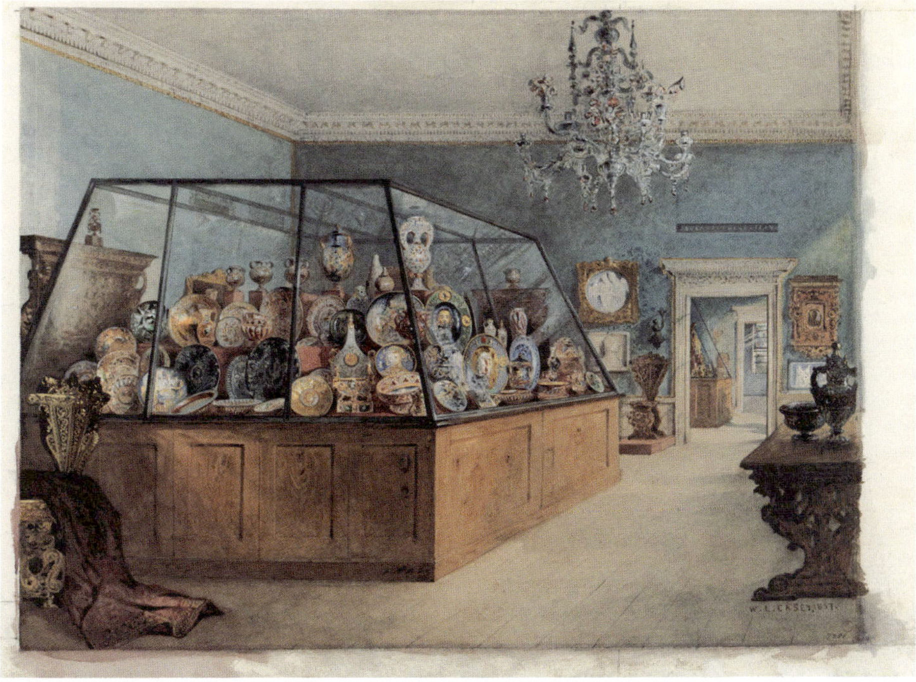

Watercolour, 1857.
7280.

The new Secretary moved swiftly to tackle the overcrowding of the Somerset House accommodation caused by the growing collection of artefacts. In April 1852 he announced the opening of a new 'Museum of Ornamental Manufactures'. This would be situated in Marlborough House, the former residence of Queen Adelaide (died 1849) in Pall Mall; its temporary use for this purpose was authorised by Queen Victoria at the request of Albert. The Prince stipulated that the collection of plaster casts and monumental art from the School of Design should be associated with his own plans to perpetuate the objectives of the Great Exhibition.

The Marlborough House Museum opened on 19 May 1852. Alongside the objects acquired by the School of Design since its opening in 1837, there were displayed the items purchased by Cole and his committee from the Great Exhibition. The visitor could marvel at 'gorgeous scarfs and shawls from Cashmere and Lahore – glittering swords, yatagans and pistols from Tunis and Constantinople – the famous 'La Gloire' vase from the Sèvres manufacture ... and other Art-illustrations of the highest order'. Cole's vision for the new Museum was of 'a schoolroom for everyone', which would instruct the public in 'good taste', both by displaying the best quality furniture, textiles, ceramics, glass and metal work, and also by contrasting these with examples of bad design. Accordingly, the corridor leading to the exhibition rooms housed a display of 'Examples of False Principles in Decoration', which came to be known as the 'Chamber of Horrors'. A particular bugbear for Cole was fabric woven with flowers and foliage. This part of the museum proved highly controversial, with loud protests coming from the manufacturers of the objects held up to ridicule. The Chamber of Horrors was soon closed down, although there were some, including the designer Christopher Dresser, who regretted its disappearance.

Andrea della Robbia (1435-1525)

Boy Playing the Bagpipes

It is thought that this exquisite statue originally formed part of an altarpiece; in style it shows similarities to winged putti on an altarpiece supplied by della Robbia to a church in Florence in 1512. The naked boy sits with the bag on his left thigh. He is blowing into the mouthpiece while fingering the chanter with both hands. This work was given by Prince Albert in 1858, at a time when the Museum was in the process of acquiring three della Robbia altarpieces from Italy.

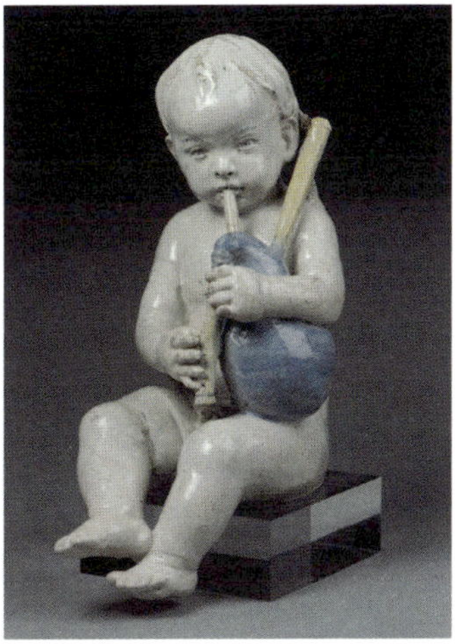

Polychrome enamelled terracotta, c.1490-1520. 4677-1858.

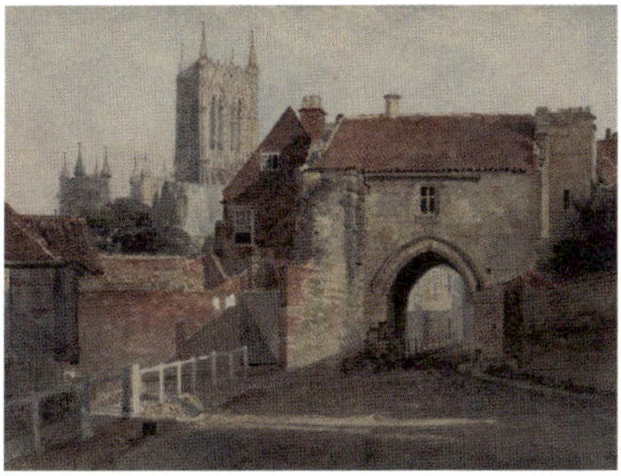

Watercolour, n.d.
P.59-1921

Peter De Wint (1784-1849)

Potter Gate, Lincoln

Peter De Wint had close connections with Lincoln through his friend, William Hilton, a native of the city who, like De Wint, was apprenticed to the London artist John Raphael Smith. In 1810 De Wint married Hilton's sister Harriet and thereafter he regularly spent the summer in Lincoln. This view of Potter Gate demonstrates De Wint's fondness for depicting one antiquity behind another. This painting was one of those given to the Museum by Mrs Tatlock, the artist's daughter.

The Gloucester Candlestick

The Gloucester Candlestick is one of the greatest treasures of the V&A and also one of its most intriguing objects. It is made of brass, but with an unusually high content of silver, and it was produced using the lost wax form of casting. The elaborate decoration is made up of figures and apes struggling amongst thick intertwining foliage. Three dragons with outspread wings form the supporting feet and the large knop (or knob) in the centre of the stem shows the symbols of the four Evangelists. An inscription tells us that it was given to the Church of St Peter in Gloucester (now Gloucester Cathedral) by Abbot Peter, who ruled between 1104-1114. It is generally agreed that the candlestick was made in England and the decoration can be closely compared with that of manuscripts made in Durham and Canterbury at this time. It also reflects the Romanesque church decoration of the so-called Hereford School, raising the possibility that it may have been made locally in the Gloucester area.

It is unusual to find medieval metalwork objects which are so securely dated and fixed within a particular area and this alone would make the candlestick especially important. The only directly comparable examples are a pair of candlesticks made for Bernward, Bishop of Hildesheim in Germany (993-1022). These are of similar form but with less elaborate decoration. Ceremonial candlesticks of this size are uncommon at this time, although there is documentary evidence for larger free-standing candlesticks being presented as gifts to important shrines. King Cnut gave a silver seven-branched candlestick to Winchester in 1035, while Christchurch, Canterbury, received a gift from its Prior, Conrad (1107-1126), of a candlestick of remarkable size made of brass, with three branches springing from the

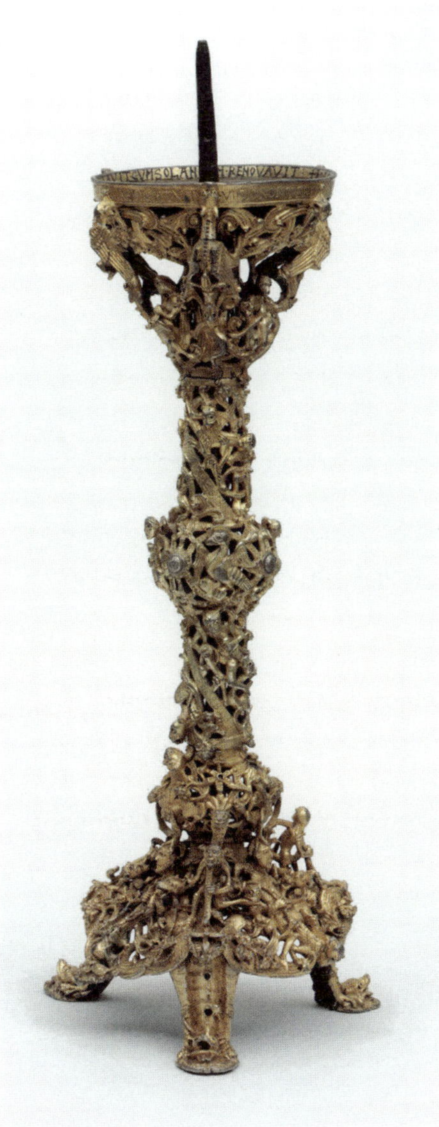

main stem on which seven candles were placed. The Gloucester Candlestick is only 52 cms high, so it seems probable that it was intended to stand upon an altar in the church, perhaps to illuminate a shrine or relics. There is an eleventh century ivory in the V&A which appears to show a candlestick placed upon an altar, but there is no documentary evidence to explain the reason for doing this.

The candlestick bears a further inscription that helps us to understand its meaning. This reads LUCIS ON(US) VIRTUTIS OPUS DOCTRINA REFULGENS PREDICAT UT VICIO NON TENEBRETUR HOMO, which can be translated This burden of light is the work of virtue, shining doctrine teaches that man be not shadowed by vice. In other words, the light of the candle is a symbol of Christ, while the decoration of the candlestick represents man's struggle against evil and sin, always reaching upwards to be to be bathed in the light of God. The idea that light was in some senses the embodiment of the Holy Spirit was common in the middle ages, especially among Benedictine communities like Gloucester. It has also been suggested that the unusual composition of the brass alloy which makes up the candlestick, with its high percentage of silver, was a deliberate attempt to produce bright surfaces which would reflect the light of the candle above.

There is one further inscription on the candlestick, which reveals its later history: Thomas of Poché gave this to the church of Le Mans, when the sun renewed the year. There is no indication of the date of this gift and Thomas de Poché has not been identified, but it has been proposed that it was in connection with the inauguration of the Cathedral of Le Mans in 1254. On this occasion there was an elaborate ceremony, in which the congregation walked thought the cathedral bearing candles as symbols of the light of Christ. It would have been entirely suitable for the Gloucester candlestick to have been presented to Le Mans for this inaugural ceremony, emphasising once again its symbolic representation of the light of God.

Whatever the precise nature of its symbolism, the Gloucester candlestick is one of the finest examples of medieval metalwork, the detail of which continues to fascinate and impress.

Alan Borg

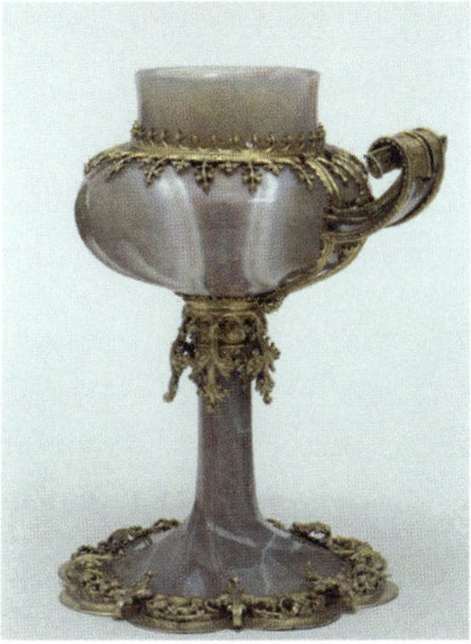

Cup, probably German: Agate, shaped and polished, with silver-gilt mounts, 19th century (in the style of c.1475). 389-1854.

Cup

This lavishly decorated cup was acquired by the Museum in 1854 for the considerable sum of £80. At the time, both Henry Cole and J. C. Robinson were eagerly searching the European art market for medieval and Renaissance objects to develop the collections of the fledgling 'Museum of Ornamental Manufactures'. This cup was regarded as a major example of late Gothic metalwork. More recent re-examination, however, has indicated that certain features of its construction – the jointed stem, separate handle and round foot disguised with a lobed mount – reveal it to be of nineteenth-century workmanship.

The new Museum soon began to outgrow its temporary quarters in Marlborough House, which in any case would need to be made available as the residence of the Prince of Wales when he attained his eighteenth birthday in 1859. Already looking for more space, Cole began to use Gore House, on the Brompton site, for temporary exhibitions. One such was a display of life drawings by William Mulready, held in 1853. The President of the Board of Trade (the Government Minister responsible for the School of Design) was shocked to see Mulready's nudes and ordered that, when the Queen visited, she was on no account to be taken into that room. The Queen, however, was not to be put off in this way, went to see the life drawings and subsequently purchased a full-length male nude study.

Cole now approached Albert, seeking a permanent home for the Museum on the 'Albertopolis' site in Brompton (or 'South Kensington' as it was becoming known). The site chosen was the dilapidated Brompton Park House and its gardens, in the south-east corner of the estate. Here the first building for the Museum was erected in 1856-7. A temporary iron structure, to save expense, it was castigated by the architectural journal, The Builder, which pronounced 'Its ugliness is unmitigated'. Its form was likened to three gigantic ship's boilers, giving rise to its popular name, the 'Brompton Boilers'. When they were eventually replaced by permanent buildings in 1872, the 'Boilers' were moved to Bethnal Green where they still form part of the structure of the V&A Museum of Childhood.

The Brompton Boilers proved to have insufficient space for the growing collection and almost immediately a northern extension was begun. This was needed to house the 'National Gallery of British Art', an important collection of works by contemporary British artists, including Turner, Constable, Landseer, Mulready, Wilkie and Crome. This collection of some 500 works had been assembled by the Yorkshire industrialist John Sheepshanks who now presented it to the nation, expressing his preference for the 'open and airy' situation of South Kensington against the pollution of central London. Like Cole, Sheepshanks was a firm believer in the importance of making art accessible to the public and his gift was conditional on a gallery being built within a year.

The 'Boilers' and the Sheepshanks Gallery were both opened in June 1857. A striking feature of the latter was its use of gas lighting. This meant that it could be opened on winter evenings, making it possible for working people to see works of art. Its architect, Francis Fowke, noted in 1858 that 'on Monday evenings ... the gallery is often visited by upwards of 3,000 people in the short space of three hours'. As Cole expressed it, 'The evening opening of public museums may furnish a powerful antidote to the gin palace'. Cole was an enthusiastic proponent of the view that museums should be easily accessible. Other museums and galleries at that time seemed to go out of their way to keep people out. The British Museum had no lavatories and therefore excluded children under eight years old (they might 'commit little indiscretions'). Its Director, Sir Henry Ellis, publicly stated that he did not want to admit 'the more vulgar class', or those 'of a very low description'. In contrast, Henry Cole won for the South Kensington Museum the honourable distinction of being the first such establishment

William Linnaeus Casey (1835-1870)

Marlborough House: First Room

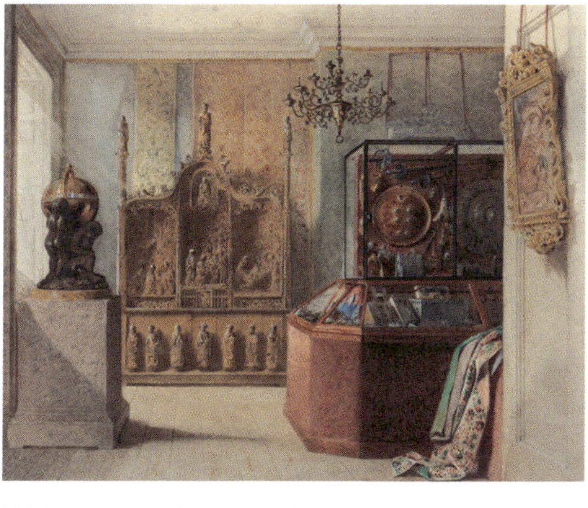

Watercolour, 1856 PDP 7279

This painting shows one of the exhibition rooms at Marlborough House as it was staged in 1856, just before the collection was moved to South Kensington. Prominently displayed on the left is the French Globe Clock, its case dating from 1783-5, while in the background can be seen the striking Altarpiece with Scenes from the Life of the Virgin (c.1520) from the Low Countries, an early example of the Museum's decision to purchase large pieces of architectural sculpture.

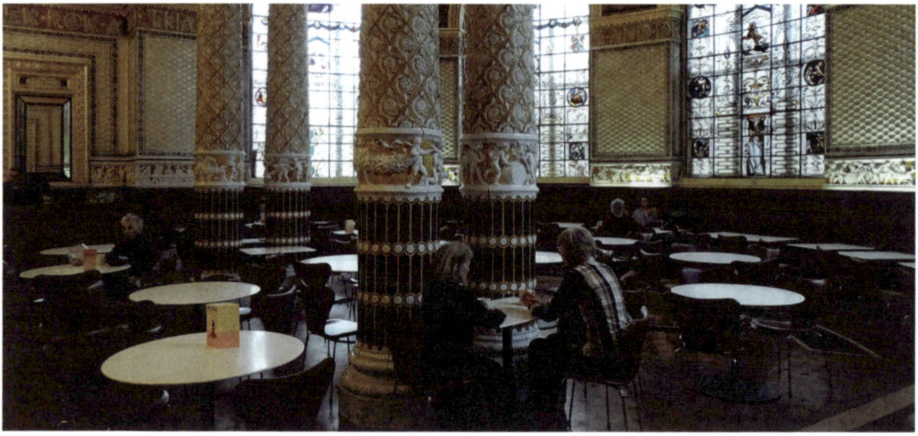

in the world to provide a restaurant for its visitors. Immediately to the right of the 'Brompton Boilers' a timber-framed building was erected in 1856. This housed the Refreshment Rooms, under the management of their proprietress, Madame Celeste. And when in 1868 the new Lecture Theatre Building opened to the public, providing a suitably impressive entrance to the Museum, visitors stepping through the magnificent bronze doors, carved with panels illustrating the marriage of Science and Art, found themselves, no doubt to their surprise, not in an exhibition hall filled with antiquities but in an attractively decorated suite of three welcoming tea rooms.

Although the presence of paintings in the South Kensington Museum undoubtedly attracted visitors, the inclusion of the National Gallery of British Art within a collection initially intended to focus on manufacture and design was not entirely logical. From 1896 the title was adopted by the new Tate Gallery on Millbank, which was to provide a new location for modern British art. Meanwhile new buildings continued to be added to the

South Kensington Museum to house a continually expanding range of collections: the Bandinel Collection of ceramics (1853), the Gherardini Collection of sculptures (1854) and, between 1855 and 1865, the Soulages, Bernal and Gigli-Campana collections. These acquisitions continued to balance contemporary with historical objects, giving the Museum its characteristic ethos. The part played in its early development by both the Queen and her husband should never be underestimated and it was entirely fitting that when in 1899 Queen Victoria, in her last public appearance, laid the foundation stone of Aston Webb's new building on Cromwell Road, the name of the institution was changed to 'The Victoria and Albert Museum'.

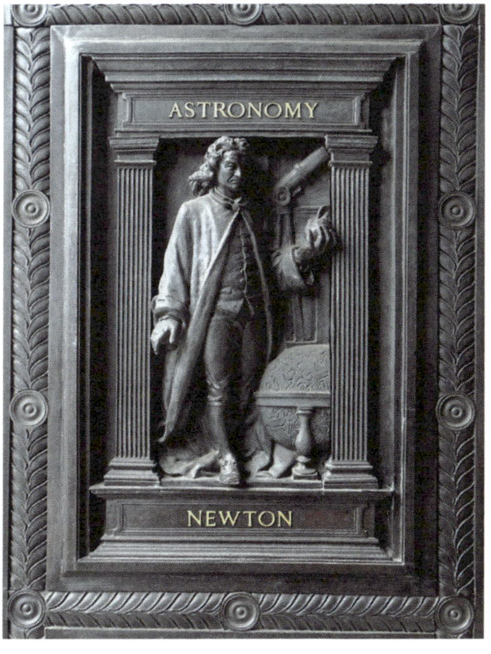

Detail from bronze entrance doors of the Lecture Theatre building (1868), showing Sir Isaac Newton.

Other Items:

Victoria

Queen Victoria *(1819-1901)*

Print depicting Islay and Eos, Victoria and Albert's pet dogs. Islay is a Skye Terrier and Eos is a Greyhound.
Etching on paper, 1840.
Prints, Drawings and Paintings: E.2176-1932

T.H.A.E. *(artist)*

The Royal Children in the Nursery. Queen Victoria and Prince Albert with their five eldest children. The Queen sits by the fireplace, with the baby Helena on her lap. The toddlers Alice and Alfred play beside her, with a garland and a small dog. Albert stands in the centre, behind a gilded armchair, watching Prince Albert Edward (wearing a sailor suit) waving a Union flag. On the chair beside him is a model boat. On the right stands Victoria, Princess Royal, with a basket of flowers on her arm. In the background on the left is an attendant in a blue dress.
Hand-coloured lithograph, 1847
Prints, Drawings and Paintings: E.834-1936

Caldesi & Montecchi
(photographers)

Queen Victoria & family on the terrace at Osborne House. The Queen has her youngest child, Princess Beatrice, on her lap. This photograph formed part of the collection of Chauncy Hare Townshend who bequeathed it to the Museum in 1868.
Albumen print from wet collodion on glass negative, 1857.
Prints, Drawings and Paintings: 68021

Charles Clifford, photographer
(1821-1863)

'Portrait of the Queen, 1861'
Shows Queen Victoria in an evening gown, wearing diamonds and a crown.
Albumen print, varnished with celluloid varnish, 1861. RPS.2992-2017

Albert

Albert, Prince Consort *(1819-1861)*

Songs and ballads: written and set to music by their Royal Highnesses Albert and Ernest, princes of Saxe-Coburg & Gotha ...
London: Henry Colburn, 1840.
National Art Library: Forster 111

'The Industrious Boy'

Punch
London: Punch Publications Limited, January-June 1850.
National Art Library: 38041800703951

Harriet Maria Smythies
(Mrs Yorick Smythies) (1813-1883)

The Prince and the people: a poem in two cantos
London: Sir Frederic Shoberl for William Skeffington, 1854.
National Art Library: 38041800136483

Manuscript

Antiquities etc. at Erbach, Hesse Darmstadt, 1859.
MSL/1860/NN2
National Art Library: 38041800971368

William Maw Egley *(1826-1916)*

The Second Christmas Card.
The sketch shows a ballroom scene on the left and a Christmas dinner on the right. Between these are a Harlequin and Columbine dancing, with the legend beneath 'Merry Christmas and a Happy New Year to You'. At the bottom left, poor people are queuing for soup. This was the preliminary drawing for the second Christmas card produced in England.
Original pencil sketch, 1848
Prints, Drawings and Paintings: E.11-1940

William Maw Egley *(1826-1916)*

Finished design for a Christmas card
Pencil on paper, 1848.
Prints, Drawings and Paintings: E.12-1940

William Maw Egley *(1826-1916)*

'The second Christmas card'.
Etching, 1848.
Prints, Drawings and Paintings: E.13-1940

The Great Exhibition

Walter Goodall *(1830-1889)*

Interior view of the Great Exhibition – 'Part of the French Court, no. 1 (Sèvres)'. In the background can be seen the display of porcelain from the Sèvres factory. The large ebony cabinet in the foreground was probably the combined work of the French firm Barbedienne & Co. and their British agents Jackson & Graham. The bronze decorations are modelled on works by Michelangelo and Ghiberti.
Watercolour on paper, 1851.
Prints, Drawings and Paintings: E.16-2007

Owen Jones *(1809-1874)*

Decoration of the transept of the Great Exhibition of 1851.
Watercolour on paper, c.1851.
Prints, Drawings and Paintings: 8270

William Wyon *(1795-1851), designer and maker*

Leonard Charles Wyon *(1826-1891), designer and maker*

Medal: Prize medal for the Great Exhibition of 1851, depicting Queen Victoria and Prince Albert. The Prize Medal was awarded to more than 2,900 exhibitors at the Exhibition. This example is inscribed to the School of Design.
Struck bronze: London, 1851.
National Art Library: 38041800799207

Anthony Carey Stannus *(1830-1919)*

'Experiments with the model of the memorial of the Exhibition of 1851. Erected in the Royal Horticultural Society's Gardens before the design was settled by H.R.H. the Prince Consort.' Depicts Prince Albert inspecting the model for the Memorial to the 1851 Exhibition, set up in the quadrangle of the South Kensington Museum. The building in the background is the Sheepshanks Gallery; the 'Brompton Boilers' can be seen to the right. Henry Cole and his dog are in the left foreground. The Memorial is now behind the Albert Hall.
Watercolour and pencil on paper, 1861.
Prints, Drawings and Paintings: 7851

Alexandre Gueyton *(1818-1862)*

Casket in 'oxidised' silver, architectural form, set with rubies and half pearls. Bought for £36 from the Great Exhibition of 1851 at which Gueyton was awarded a Council Medal.
Oxidised silver and silver-gilt, set with rubies and pearls, Paris, ca.1851.
Metalwork Collection: 155-1852

Francis Bedford *(1816-1894)*

Photograph attributed to Francis Bedford, depicting a hunting knife made by Marrel and probably displayed at the Great Exhibition.
Albumen print, c.1855-1860.
Prints, Drawings and Paintings: E.432-1995

The South Kensington Museum

R. W. Herman

Study of ornament from a plaster cast. Students at the Government School of Design were taught the principles of good design by the study of plaster casts of classical sculptures and architectural ornament. Prizes were awarded for outstanding work. This drawing won the first prize ever offered by the School for drawing ornament from the cast.
Black and white chalks on buff paper, 1840
Prints, Drawings and Paintings: E.1967-1909

Jennens and Bettridge

(manufacturer)

Tray with a detail of Landseer's painting 'Bolton Castle in Olden Time', depicting a huntsman returning and a cook with a fish. This may have been the tray included in Henry Cole's 'False Principles' exhibition at Marlborough House in 1852, selected because of the incongruous combination of painting and border. It may also be the tray alluded to by Charles Dickens in his review of the exhibition, 'A House Full of Horrors', published later that year.
Papier mâché, painted, gilded and inlaid with mother-of-pearl, c.1850.
Furniture and Woodwork Collection: W.6-1920

William Wyon, designer and maker *(1795-1851)*

Medal

Prince Albert's Medal depicting Prince Albert and St George and the Dragon. A gold version of the Personal Medal for HRH Prince Albert: this example was presented by the Prince to Henry Cole as a memorial of their joint achievements. Cole later bequeathed it to the Museum.
Struck gold: London, 1845.
National Art Library: 38041800799231

Workbox

Lacquerware: 6 parts inside.
Given by HM Queen Victoria.
Domestic, wood, lacquered painted, Lahore, 19th century.
South and South East Asia Collection: 2-1852

Writing case

Lacquered wood, possibly Kashmir or Lahore, c.1850.
South and South East Asia Collection: 4:1-1852

Königliche Porzellan Manufaktur Berlin

Figure of King Frederick William III of Prussia, with stand.
Given by HRH The Prince Consort.
White biscuit porcelain, 19th century.
Ceramics: 4740&A-1858

Bowl

Hard-paste porcelain bowl, of moulded five lobe shape, painted in enamels with a Japanese style design, made by the Meissen porcelain factory, Germany.
Given by HM Queen Victoria.
Hard-paste porcelain, moulded, painted in enamels, 1729-31. Ceramics: 7327-1860

Bowl

Porcelain bowl with scalloped edge, decorated with flowers and birds in imitation of Japanese Imari porcelain.
Given by HM Queen Victoria.
Porcelain, painted in overglaze enamels and gilt.
China, Qing dynasty, 1700-1730.
East Asia Collection: 7338-1860

Bowl

Porcelain bowl, fluted with scalloped edge. Painted in overglaze enamels with compartments containing flowers.
Given by HM Queen Victoria.
Porcelain, painted in overglaze enamels.
Jingdezhen, 1700-1730.
East Asia Collection: 7337-1860

Box

Domed box. Decorative papier mâché was made in Kashmir for both local and European markets.
Given by HM Queen Victoria.
Papier mâché, painted and varnished,
Srinagar, Kashmir, c.1850
South and South East Asia Collection: 3-1852

Charles Thurston Thompson, photographer *(1816-1868)*

Photograph of a French cabinet owned by Isambard Kingdom Brunel.
From a set of photographs of Decorative Chairs at the Exhibition of Ancient Furniture (held at Gore House, Kensington in 1852) and the Soulages Collection.
Prints, Drawings and Paintings: 33573

Charles Thurston Thompson, photographer *(1816-1868)*

Photograph from a set of photographs of Decorative Chairs at the Exhibition of Ancient Furniture (held at Gore House, Kensington in 1852) and the Soulages Collection.
Prints, Drawings and Paintings: 33565

Charles Thurston Thompson, photographer *(1816-1868)*

'Carved oak chair, Italian work, date 1530-50.'
Photograph from a set of photographs by Charles Thurston Thompson of the Soulages Collection.
Prints, Drawings and Paintings: 33434

Charles Thurston Thompson, photographer *(1816-1868)*

Photograph: 'Mirror, date about 1660-70 from Knole'.
Albumen print, 1853.
Prints, Drawings and Paintings: 39793

Michelangelo *(1475-1564)*

Statuette 'Dawn', copy after marble figure by Michelangelo in the Medici Chapel, Florence.
Terracotta, painted in dark bronze colour, 16th century.
Sculpture Collection: 4119-1854

Plaque

Horizontal rectangular copper-gilt plaque. This originally formed part of a chasse, or reliquary casket, made in Limoges and depicting the martyrdom of St Thomas Becket at Canterbury Cathedral in 1170. The animated poses of the two knights contrast with the still figure of the Archbishop.
Copper-gilt, champlevé enamel, 1190-1210.
Metalwork Collection: 4041-1856

Alexandre Gueyton *(1818-1862)*

Elkington & Co.
This casket was bought in 1854 from Elkington & Co. of Birmingham. It is an exact copy of a silver casket by the French silversmith Alexandre Gueyton, which was displayed at the Great Exhibition in 1851. The Museum acquired the original casket and later added the copy as a teaching aid for students at the Government School of Design.
Electrotype: copper, silvered and oxidised, c.1854
Metalwork Collection: REPRO.1854D-40

Caspar Lehmann *(engraver)*

Rectangular glass panel. Bohemian glass was highly prized and Caspar Lehmann was one of the greatest master engravers.
Given by HRH The Prince Consort.
Glass, engraved, Prague, 1620.
Ceramics Collection: 6939-1860

Caspar Lehmann *(engraver)*

'Perseus and Andromeda'. Rectangular glass panel, engraved, probably Bohemia (Prague), possibly Germany (Dresden).
Given by HRH The Prince Consort.
Glass, engraved, 1607-1611.
Ceramics Collection: 6940-1860

Caspar Lehmann *(engraver)*

Engraved glass panel, Bohemia (Prague). The imagery appears to connect it with Christian II, Elector of Saxony, and his wife Hedwig.
Given by HRH The Prince Consort.
Glass, engraved, 1619.
Ceramics Collection: 6938-1860

Anthony Carey Stannus *(1830-1919)*

Topographical view of Brompton Park House (demolished after 1901).
Watercolour, 1863.
Prints, Drawings and Paintings: 2813

Godfrey Sykes *(1824-1866)*

Francis Fowke *(1823-1865)*

Drawing of the frontage of the Lecture Theatre at the South Kensington Museum. Design in red, brown and grey watercolour for the centre portion of the north side of the quadrangle.
Watercolour on paper, about 1865
Prints, Drawings and Paintings: D.930-1899

Photograph

Minutolisches Institut Liegnitz; Anon, Stoneware jugs/tankards,German/ Netherlandish
The collection assembled by the Prussian civil servant Baron Alexander von Minutoli (1806-1887) formed the basis of the Minutolisches Institut in Liegnitz (now Legnica in Poland), which aimed to improve the quality of local manufactured goods through the study of decorative arts - an ambition shared by Prince Albert and Henry Cole in Great Britain.
19th century.
Prints, Drawings and Paintings: 36018

Photograph

Minutolisches Institut Liegnitz; Anon, Vases & dish.
19th century.
Prints, Drawings and Paintings: 35964

Minutolischen Institut zur Veredlung der Gewerbe und Beförderung der Künste (Liegnitz)
Vorbilder für Handwerker und Fabrikanten aus den Sammlungen des Minutolischen Instituts... zu Liegnitz.
Liegnitz, 1855.
National Art Library: 38041005064613

J. N. Fuchs *(1774-1856)* and Frédéric Kuhlmann *(1803-1881)*

Bound volume comprising three works on water-glass:
On the applications of water-glass (soluble alkaline silicate) in the arts, by Frédéric Kuhlmann.
London: Taylor and Francis, 1859.
On the manufacture, properties, and application of water-glass (soluble alkaline silicate), by J. N. Fuchs.
London: Taylor and Francis, 1859.
Bereitung, Eigenschaften und Nutzauswendung des Wasserglasses, by J. N Fuchs.
München: Literarisch-artische Anstalt, 1857.
National Art Library: 38041800367740

Charles Thurston Thompson, photographer *(1816-1868)*

'Exhibition of the Photographic Society of London and the Societe Francaise de Photographie at the South Kensington Museum'.
Copy print.
TNN.166-2018 (copy print of 2715-1913)

The National Gallery of British Art

William Mulready *(1786-1863)*

Study for a portrait of John Sheepshanks. The collector John Sheepshanks is portrayed in his house in New Bond Street, surrounded by his books and portfolios, while his housekeeper brings his letters.
Pen and sepia on paper, 1832. FA.75

William Mulready *(1786-1863)*

Life study: female half figure, dressing her hair.
Chalk on paper, 1849.
Prints, Drawings and Paintings: 6577

William Mulready *(1786-1863)*

Life study: male figure, seated, holding his leg.
Chalk on paper, 1861-2.
Prints, Drawings and Paintings: 6592

William Mulready *(1786-1863)*

Life study: male figure, seated.
Chalk on paper, mid 19th century.
Prints, Drawings and Paintings: 6602

William Mulready *(1786-1863)*

Female nude sitting on the floor.
Given by John Sheepshanks.
Chalk drawing on paper, early 19th century.
Prints, Drawings and Paintings: FA.74

Sir Edwin Landseer *(1802-1873)*

'A Fireside Party'. Five dogs warm themselves on a hearth.
Given by John Sheepshanks, 1857.
Oil on panel, 1829.
Prints, Drawings and Paintings: FA.90(O)

Sir Edwin Landseer *(1802-1873)*

'Tethered Rams'. Two rams and two sheepdogs in the foreground are set in a landscape of mountains and a lake.
Given by John Sheepshanks, 1857.
Oil on panel, c.1839.
Prints, Drawings and Paintings: FA.95(O)

Peter De Wint *(1784-1849)*

'Old Houses on the High Bridge, Lincoln'.
Oil on millboard, early 19th century.
Bequeathed by Miss Harriet Helen Tatlock, granddaughter of the artist.
Prints, Drawings and Paintings: P.58-1921

William Mulready *(1786-1863)*

'Near the Mall, Kensington Gravel Pits'. This area is now known as Notting Hill Gate. The artist lived here from around 1811; the area was noted for its fresh unpolluted air.
Given by John Sheepshanks, 1857.
Oil on canvas, c.1812.
Prints, Drawings and Paintings: FA.135(O)

William Mulready *(1786-1863)*

'The Mall, Kensington Gravel Pits'.
Exhibited at the Royal Academy 1844.
Given by John Sheepshanks, 1857.
Oil on canvas, c.1812.
Prints, Drawings and Paintings: FA.136(O)

David Roberts *(1796-1864)*

'Entrance to the Crypt, Roslin Chapel'.
Given by John Sheepshanks, 1857.
Oil on panel, 1843.
Prints, Drawings and Paintings: FA.174(O)

Sir Augustus Wall Callcott *(1779-1844)*

The painting depicts cows with the Dutch town of Dort or Dordrecht in the background. The artist's picturesque style is influenced by the Dutch tradition.
Given by John Sheepshanks, 1857.
Oil on panel, 1841.
Prints, Drawings and Paintings: FA.11(O)

Friedrich Gauermann *(1807-1862)*

Oil painting entitled 'Wild boars and wolf'.
Given by John Sheepshanks:
Gauermann was the only foreign artist represented in the Sheepshanks gift.
His work was particularly admired by Prince Albert when he visited the newly-opened Sheepshanks Gallery in 1857.
Oil on canvas, 1835.
Prints, Drawings and Paintings: FA.78(O)

Peter De Wint *(1784-1849)*

Lincoln Cathedral.
This was one of forty-nine works bequeathed to the Museum by Mrs Richard Ellison of Sudbrooke Holme, Lincoln. These were in addition to the fifty-one watercolours which she had given in 1860, the whole collection forming the Ellison Gift.
Watercolour, 1841.
Prints, Drawings and Paintings: 1021-1873

Sir Edwin Landseer *(1802-1873)*

'The Twa Dogs': this painting of a Newfoundland dog and a collie illustrates the poem of that name by Robert Burns.
Given by John Sheepshanks, 1857.
Oil on canvas, 1822.
Prints, Drawings and Paintings: FA.92(O)

Charles West Cope *(1811-1890)*

'Mother and Child'. Cope was a Roman Catholic and the mother and child was a subject to which he returned many times.
Given by John Sheepshanks, 1857.
Oil on gesso on canvas, 1852.
Prints, Drawings and Paintings: FA.60(O)

Sir Edwin Landseer *(1802-1873)*

'The Old Shepherd's Chief Mourner'. This painting was exhibited at the Royal Academy in 1837. and was a popular success.
Given by John Sheepshanks, 1857.
Oil on canvas, 1837.
Prints, Drawings and Paintings: FA.93(O)

Peter De Wint *(1784-1849)*

'Haymaking'.
Given by Mrs P. Tatlock, daughter of the artist.
Oil on canvas, about 1815-1830.
Prints, Drawings and Paintings: 260-1872

Sir David Wilkie *(1785-1841)*

'The Refusal'. Wilkie's painting illustrates the song 'Duncan Gray' by Robert Burns. At first, proud Maggie refuses Duncan's proposal of marriage but later changes her mind. The artist William Mulready was the model for Duncan.
Given by John Sheepshanks, 1857.
Oil on panel, 1814.
Prints, Drawings and Paintings: FA.226(O)

Joseph Mallord William Turner *(1775-1851)*

'Life-Boat and Manby Apparatus Going off to a Stranded Vessel Making Signal (Blue Lights) of Distress'. The Manby apparatus was a life-saving device invented by Captain George Manby after a shipwreck in 1807 off Great Yarmouth (thought to have been the setting for this painting). It consisted of a rope fired from a mortar.
Given by John Sheepshanks, 1857.
Oil on canvas, c.1831.
Prints, Drawings and Paintings: FA.211(O)

John Constable *(1776-1837)*

A Watermill at Gillingham, Dorset.
Bequeathed by Isabel Constable, 1888.
Oil on canvas, 1823-1827
Prints, Drawings and Paintings: 1632-1888

Sir Edwin Landseer *(1802-1873)* Comical Dogs

The Sheepshanks Collection of contemporary British paintings, given to the Museum in 1857, included a group of works by Landseer. The artist was particular celebrated for his animal paintings. Despite the bizarre costume and accessories, these two wire-haired terriers retain their canine character. The dog on the left wears a Scottish bonnet and has a ram's horn snuff box under his paw; the other animal has a white lady's cap and seems to smoke a pipe.

John Constable *(1776-1837)* The Cottage in a Cornfield

It is thought that Constable began this painting about 1817, basing the donkey in the foreground on a life study done in 1815. However, the work remained unfinished until 1833 when he exhibited it at the Royal Academy. The contrast between the ripe corn to the right of the cottage and the green corn in the shadier part of the field suggests that harvest time has not yet arrived. This painting formed part of the significant bequest of Constable's works made to the Museum in 1888 by Miss Isabel Constable, the painter's last surviving daughter.

PICTURE CREDITS

The Winterhalter portrait of Queen Victoria with Prince Albert Edward is reproduced by kind permission of Royal Collection Trust/ © Her Majesty Queen Elizabeth II 2019. The Denning portrait of Princess Victoria aged Four is reproduced by permission of Dulwich Picture Gallery, London. Photographs on pages 7, 9, 27, 50 and 51 are by the author. All other images are ©Victoria and Albert Museum, London.

We wish to record our thanks to our sponsors:
Lincoln City Council
Investors in Lincoln
The University of Lincoln
Lincolnshire Co-operative Society
Brewin Dolphin
J. Owen Day & Co and Ralph Day & Co
Denby Transport
The Lindum Group
Baroness Hogg
Mr C. Howard
Mr and Mrs M. Jolly
Mr and Mrs J. Lockwood
Omex Agriculture
James Usher & Sons Ltd

We are also grateful to all those who have anonymously sponsored the Exhibition and made kind donations towards it.